WITHER GLOBALIZATION ENTER

CONNECTEDNESS

BY

GEOFFREYSON KHAMALA

i

Published by:

ISBN-13: 978-1505243925

ISBN-10: 1505243920

DEDICATION

I dedicate this book to the nonprofit sector. Henceforth the

nonprofit sector will play a decisive role in complementing the

state and private sector in shaping the direction and

momentum of global integration

TABLE OF CONTENTS

LIST OF ACRONYMS & ABBREVIATIONS

BCE   –   Before Common Era

CE   -   Common Era

DNA   –   Deoxyribonucleic Acid

EPR paradox -   Einstein–Podolsky–Rosen paradox

etc.   -   et cetera

GPS   -   The Global Positioning System

GPS   -   Global Positioning System

i.e.   -   that is

ICC   -   The International Criminal Court

NGOs   -   Non-Governmental Organizations

UN   -   United Nations

US   -   United States

USSR   -   The Union of Soviet Socialist Republics

PUBLICATIONS BY GEOFFREYSON KHAMALA

1. The Perfect Theory: A Complete Unified Description of the Universe (2014)

2. What is science? Science as an Adaptive Capacity (2014)

3. Is Science Religion? (2014)

4. Wither Globalization Enter Connectedness (2014)

5. The Ultimate Theory: The Perfect Description of the Universe (2015)

6. Tajiriba Spaces: The Solution to Sub-Optimal Outcomes (2015)

7. Zero Unemployment in Kenya: The Utility of Tajiriba Spaces (2015)

8. Reclaiming the Sahara: A Case for Universal Connectedness (2015)

ABSTRACT

For countless millennia, relatedness has been the fulcrum of world politics, economics, society, psychology and technology.

In this write-up, I demonstrate why and how globalization (a form of relatedness) is being replaced by connectedness as manifest in the way humanity organizes itself politically, economically, socially and emotionally.

The world is herein best understood in terms of spatial position (space) and non-spatial relationships. Spatial dimensions simply refer to physical objects, geography and location. Non-spatial dimensions connect us with the rest of the universe in non-physical realms. Non-spatial dimensions include gravity, electromagnetism, strong nuclear interaction, weak nuclear interaction, dark matter, dark energy, mental faculties, senses, emotions, time, life and death. This is on the understanding that, with no discernible edge to the cosmos, the universe is extended infinitely.

Therefore, the universe is an infinitely extended point. In an infinite universe, every point (location) in non-Euclidean space can be regarded as the center of the universe.

Humans and other life-forms evolve, practice and learn to manipulate phenomena (physical and non-physical phenomena) to stay alive. Human socio-political and economic configurations and the subsequent terrestrial squabbles informed by relatedness are frequently driven by the fear of death but ordinarily manifest as struggles for supremacy, resources and mating partners.

Connectedness represents a sustainable form of global integration made possible by increased human awareness of our bond with the rest of the universe, and the consequent capacity to transform nature through relentless invention, innovation and deployment of new technologies to simplify daily lives and transform humanity by facilitating the collapse of natural and artificial boundaries across the world.

Unlike globalization, connectedness (global connectivity and togetherness) represents the total collapse of boundaries and divisions in the human society in the quest to protect life.

Admirably, it appears both inanimate and animate realms have always conspired to constantly sustain life. And as life-forms manage to withstand extremes, chances are that, endless life may be achieved. So far, only the jellyfish is capably undying.

Keywords: Globalization, connectedness, relatedness, non-spatial dimensions, sustainable integration

CHAPTER ONE

THE QUEST FOR SUSTAINABLE GLOBAL INTEGRATION

INTRODUCTION

Globalization and connectedness[1] are separate and distinct conceptual frameworks to think about the world. Francis Fukuyama's contention that globalization marks the finale of the progress of human thought has attracted widespread and lasting interest but this write-up proposes that connectedness is emerging as the focal point of politics, economics, society, science and technology.

Humans constantly adapt to the changing environments around them to stay alive. The emergence of the state (and other socio-political and economic configurations) is part of the universe's evolution to guarantee our existence. The state as a spatial entity facilitates the sustenance of life (i.e. public security, safety and welfare) within a defined geographical jurisdiction. States exist to protect life. Not vice versa. However, states are involved in a global power struggle as a result of relatedness[2].

---

[1] Connectedness refers to global togetherness based on a shared cause; shared prosperity and collective existence.

1

Competing identities (lineage and descent groups, clans, ethnic groups, religions, races and civilizations) interfere with the states' capacities to fulfill the universe's will.

Relatedness contributes to the accumulation of mistrust, hatred, frustration and false pride. Relatedness is the reason as to why the people's will (the popular will or will of the majority) frequently diverts from the will of the universe.

States have been manipulated by these contending identities to build walls of separation, discrimination and hatred. The inability of state units to pursue global inclusivity and societal good is energizing the rise of global togetherness.

The global community has the responsibility to assist states to fulfill their primary responsibility of excising public authority to protect life (i.e. guarantee peacefulness, provide security, and improve livelihoods through the provision of .indispensable public goods).

A wind of change is sweeping across the world. Soon there will be no borders separating countries. The improvement in transport is integrating places, improving market access, and encouraging spatial agglomeration. The Internet connectivity

---

[2] Relatedness refers to politics along fault lines of lineage and descent groups, clans, ethnic groups, religions, races and civilizations.

and social networks are collapsing boundaries by connecting people, events, processes and places.

The ascendancy of global connectedness is beckoning. Decision-making, resource allocation, and enterprise is being devolved worldwide. Progressively global diplomacy may well be conducted by and on behalf of a global network of sustainable (inclusive and outward looking) neighborhoods.

Forward-looking non-state actors are leading the way by facilitating the rise of a global citizenry, a common goal and value system with a worldwide appeal while shunning identity struggles, territorial disputes and other differences informed by old animosities.

The nonprofit sector is scaling up its efforts to compliment states and the private sector in urbanizing remote locations around the world to guarantee humanity dignified work, education, healthcare and infrastructure.

GLOBALIZATION AS A FORM OF RELATEDNESS

Globalization has generated admiration and anger in equal measures. This is basically because globalization can be understood in two important ways. Globalization can be understood in the context of world integration as in global institutions and processes (Sassen, 2003: 1). However, globalization is frequently understood as the triumph of Western dominance in the context of the Cold War matrix (Fukuyama, 1992).

So, globalization is an intellectual movement toward political, economic, financial, trade, cultural and communications integration of different parts of the world under the armpit of 'The West'. The movements' major assumption is that as ideas, knowledge, capital, goods and services move more easily around the globe, the experiences of people around the world become more similar (read 'Western').

This explains why it is common to come across phrases such as 'western tradition', 'western canon', 'western influence', 'western knowledge', 'western media', 'western sources', 'western democracy', 'westernization', 'western civilization' or simply 'The West'.

Understood this way, globalization exacerbates inequality, competition and division, and as such, does not represent the best route to achieving a truly global village.

History has taught us that relatedness leads to a ruinous and perilous destination. Relatedness manifests in the human society as contestations within and between families, lineages, clans, castes, ethnicities, nation-states, races, religions, and civilizations.

Imperialism is the foreign control of resources and decision-making. External control of assets and the allocation of value may formal (formal empire) or informal (informal empire).

Forms of imperialism (slavery, colonialism and apartheid, neo-colonialism and globalization) are some of the byproducts of relatedness.

The four major phases of imperialism are pre-modern period (pre 1500 CE) and early modern period (1500 – 1800 CE) classical or old imperialism (that includes slavery) (pre 1800 CE); 19th century and early 20th century new imperialism (colonialism) (1850s -1945 CE); 20th century neo-colonialism (flag independence) (1945 – 1990 CE); and 21st century globalization (1991 CE - ?). Globalization is the latest phase of imperialism (Waltz, 2000; Amin, 2003; Chomsky, 2003).

Imperialism involves the exercise of formal or informal power but is every so often equated with international belligerence. This explains why Neoliberalism (or globalization theory/Washington Consensus) has been met with stiff public resistance worldwide.

Critics of globalization suggest that the world deserve better (Stiglitz, 2001; Perkins, 2004; Bakan, 2005). The global justice movement advocate for alternative forms of global integration that better support human rights, fair trade, democracy and sustainable development (Juris, 2008; Hosseini, 2009).

Globalization is the continuation of lose-lose struggle for existence. Competition among social groups is a mild form of war which regularly explodes into open violent conflict in desperate attempts to change the status quo.

In all probability, polarity (unipolarity/hegemony, bipolarity, tripolarity or multipolarity) is not the best way to organize the world society.

History is replete with failed attempts to establish parochial domination: the Athenian pride in the superiority of their civilization that led to Persian and Peloponnesian wars; Alexander's machinations and campaigns (336-323 BCE); Romans' wars of conquest and expansion; Napoleonic wars; Hitler's misguided attempt to rule the world leading to WWII; European colonialism leading to self-determination wars; the Cold War supremacy contest between the US and the USSR; and global terrorism as a reaction to perceived domination by 'The West'.

Historically attempts to establish a hegemon have failed. The imperial history of the Romans, Chinese, Spanish, Ottoman, Japanese, and British empires attests to this reality.

The United States of America, the current prospective hegemon, seems to be withdrawing from the contention for greatness without a replacement in sight.

Amid the hype of China's rise, China is incapable or doesn't want to shoulder the burdens of global overstretch.

Russia lacks the economic vitality, the military muscle and, most importantly, a rallying value system to take the place of the US.

The US's diminishing supremacy in virtually every part of the world is because Americans are wary of ambitious new foreign (military) engagements following the experience during the major wars, Korea, Somalia, Iraq and Afghanistan.

In view of this, globalization is giving room to the ascendancy of connectedness. The cancer of relatedness is being overcome daily.

CONNECTEDNESS ENVISIONS SUSTAINABLE INTEGRATION

For millennia, relatedness has been the fulcrum of world politics. Humans have for ages been socialized to be indifferent to the sufferings of fellow beings separated from them by boundaries of religion, ethnicity, race, citizenship, caste, creed and civilization.

The transition from human bands, tribal confederacies, chiefdoms, dynastic kingdoms, empires to state societies is littered with bloody struggles and supremacy contests.

Today, world politics is shaped by historical fears, insecurities and hatreds informed by past experiences of atrocities and other injustices.

Relatedness explains why states arm, spy, sabotage and compete for stature, power and wealth. Because of relatedness, the world's best scientists end up working on deadly weaponry. Sadly, today humans have even threatened their very existence by concocting chemical and biological weapons, spreading robotic warfare, developing nuclear weapons and engaging in cyber warfare. Indisputably, there is an inherent danger in structuring the world into categories that polarize society into 'us versus them'.

Connectedness is the attempt to restructure politics, economics and the human society to remedy the relatedness dilemma.

Relatedness is exclusive, divisive and conflict-ridden while connectedness is inclusive, collaborative, forward-looking and value-laden. Relatedness thrives on boundaries, discrimination, individualism, pointless competition and perilous showdowns while connectedness blurs boundaries, bigotry and is favour of consensus-building, agenda-setting and collaboration.

Whereas relatedness is premised on human insecurity and fear of untimely death connectedness is premised on hope, mutual benefit and a shared goal. According to Connectedness, perpetual life is possible, even likely.

Connectedness is a unique way of thinking that is set to transform and re-engineer human relationships and the way the world society is organized politically, economically and socially. Connectedness involves a change in the way humanity experiences localness and understand geography. The world is coming to the realization that identifying with a larger principle is far more important than belonging to multiple exclusive antagonistic identities. Evidently, the universe is struggling to transcend relatedness.

Sustainable integration of the world is best achieved through a shared goal and value system, collaboration, cooperation, information sharing and self-criticism (connectedness) rather than the pursuit of self-interest, division, boundaries, exclusion, discrimination and competition (relatedness).

Humanity is embracing connectedness reflecting the realization that our respective journeys are purpose-driven. This reality is prominently demonstrated by the emergence of global institutions and processes principally the formation of the UN, the codification of human rights, and the establishment of the International Criminal Court (ICC), the rise of civil society, the stoppage of slavery, the end of colonialism, the invention of the Internet, the rise of social media, advances is curative and preventive medicine, the spread of democracy and the emergence of a global citizenry.

Sterilization, cannibalism, infanticide, killing of twins, human sacrifice, slave sacrifice, headhunting, dueling, geronticide, lynching, trial by ordeal and capital punishment have been (or are on the verge of being) moralized out of existence.

Social behaviours such as cattle rustling, ethnic animosities, nuclear arms races and other supremacy battles are slowly being discarded. Majority of the people are turned off by terror tactics involving violence, suicide killings and mass bombings.

Humanity is recurrently becoming disgusted with violent and blood-letting behaviours. The question becomes why? These behaviors are out of synch with the law of the universe.

CONCLUSION

Relatedness, which is premised on boundaries of family line, lineage, clan, ethnicity, faith, race and civilizational jingoism, is being replaced with connectedness. Connectedness represents sustainable global integration.

CHAPTER TWO

CONNECTEDNESS AS A WAY OF THEORIZING THE UNIVERSE HOLISTICALLY

INTRODUCTION

Until recently, the quest to explain everything has been solely the preoccupation of theoretical physicists. Connectedness is an innovative way to codify scientific knowledge from the natural sciences, the humanities and everyday experience. Connectedness effortlessly explains the totality of the phenomenal world.

HOW THE UNIVERSE WAS UNDERSTOOD BEFORE CONNECTEDNESS

Since the prehistoric times, humans have been curious to comprehend the world around them. Some of the early arguments and debates over nature of the universe include Heraclitus (everything changes), Parmenides (nothing ever changes), Anaxagoras (everything is infinitely divisible), Leucippus and Democritus (Atomic Theory - the supposition that everything in the universe is either atoms or voids),

Socrates (dialectical method/eternal forms), Plato (idealism/forms and ideas) and Aristotle (empiricism).

Later Newtonian Mechanics conceptualized the universe in terms of particles and absolute space giving the world gravity (Westfall, 2007). Isaac Newton (1643 – 1727 CE) was among the first people to demonstrate that the natural world is governed by universal laws. Newton in his Theory of Gravitation demonstrated that every mass pulls at every other mass with a force comparative to the product of their masses and inversely relative to the square of the distance separating them. But Newtonian Physics could not explain the possibility for something to act upon another at a distance through emptiness without the intervention of anything else. The problem of action-at-a-distance later found explanation in Albert Einstein's General Theory of Relativity.

Before Albert Einstein (1879–1955) came along, Euclid (330 BCE) in *The Elements* discovered Euclidean flat space geometry (Euclid, 2002). Euclid observed that a point is dimensionless, a straight line is one-dimensional, a plane is two-dimensional and finally space is three-dimensional. Euclid supposed that his axioms were self-evident statements about the everyday world around us.

Following Euclid, René Descartes (1596-1650 CE) discovered an abstract way of conceptualizing the physical world using the right angle (the Cartesian plane) (Grayling, 2005).

Today we express the universe as being three-dimensional thanks to the Cartesian/Analytic Geometry. Descartes used algebra to describe three-dimensional geometry, where every point in Euclidean space is represented by an ordered triple of coordinates (x, y, z).

Before Descartes, monists held that the mind is not something separate from the body; the mind is all that exists and the external world is either mental itself, or an illusion created by the mind. Descartes distinguished between the realm of thought and the realm of matter. He was the first to clearly identify the mind with consciousness and self-awareness.

Descartes demonstrated that consciousness (the mind) can exist independently of physical reality (e.g. the brain). Accordingly, to appropriately grasp the universe one has to develop a few simple, fundamental ideas of reality from which geometrical deduction of more complex ideas and theories emerges.

Immanuel Kant (1724-1804 CE) in his work *Critique of Pure Reason* (1781) noted that the phenomenal world (phenomena) should be the subject for scientific study because the *noumenal* (true) world (the thing-in-itself) is not knowable (Kant, 1848). According to Kant, the mind plays a central role in influencing the way that the world is experienced.

In Kantian terms, sensory and mental representations are mere phenomena. We explain the world using mental concepts such as space and time, which are not substances but a priori particulars that enable us to comprehend sense experience. Substances are the basic things out of which the world is composed.

Arthur Schopenhauer (1788 – 1860 CE) in *The World as Will and Representation* (1818) divided the universe into will and representation (Schopenhauer, 1958). He believed that we could gain knowledge about the thing-in-itself. Will, for Schopenhauer, is what Kant called the 'thing-in-itself'. For him, self-preservation is the overriding motivation among human beings and all observable phenomena. Therefore, the entire universe and everything in it as driven by a primordial desire to avoid death.

Schopenhauer has since been labeled the foremost pessimist for concluding that human desire and action is illogical, directionless and self-defeating.

Gottfried Leibniz anticipated Albert Einstein by arguing, against Newton, that space, distance, time and motion are relative, not absolute (Antognazza, 2008).

Einstein invented differential geometry when he extended his Special Theory of Relativity to encompass Newton's theory of gravitation with the end result being *General Theory of Relativity*.

For Einstein (2010), gravitation is not force acting at a distance as Newton had suggested but the outcome of the curvature of space and time. This means that gravity can be explained in terms of geometry, rather than as interacting forces. For Einstein, reality is spatial and temporal dimensions[3] or simply space-time.

Scientists observe that Einstein's General Relativity is about the largest things in the universe and falters in attempts to fathom the behavior and interaction of elementary particles. Subsequently, Quantum Mechanics deals with nature at the atomic and subatomic levels. But fitting Gravity (macroscopic realm) comfortably into the Standard Framework (microscopic realm) has proved to be a difficult challenge. The Standard Model apparently does not completely explain the

[3] Dimensions are basically the distinctive aspects of what we make out to be reality as we know it.

nature of the universe. Einstein and his colleagues (EPR Paradox) also concluded that Quantum Theory could not be a final theory of nature (Einstein *et al.*, 1935; Selleri, 1988).

The other dilemma is that Expansion Theory suggests that the universe is not only expanding but that its expansion rate is increasing (Perlmutter *et al.*, 1999). The theory predicts that the universe will expand forever at an even faster rate due to dark energy. The implication is that the universe is composed of 5% normal matter (protons, neutrons and electrons), 23% dark matter and 72% antigravity dark energy.

Dark energy and cosmic acceleration are a failure of General Relativity on very large scales. However, the fact that 95% of physical reality is literally obscure, comprising of dark matter and dark energy, has not stopped scientists in the quest to elucidate every single aspect of the universe in one theory in attempts to describe all known observable fundamental interactions at both sub-atomic (quantum mechanics) and cosmological scales (stars, planets, galaxies) (Weinberg, 1993; Ellis, 2000).

Candidate theories of everything such as string theories have postulated the existence of additional hidden spatial dimensions of reality (Marshall, 2010). String Theory requires the existence of extra dimensions beyond the three (length, width and depth) we know about. The theory suggests that matter is made of minuscule vibrating threads of energy (Musser, 2008). However, the existence of more than four dimensions would only appear to make a difference at the subatomic level. Further, finding a way to confirm String Theory with our current technology is a major challenge. Further still, quantum gravity theories assume, and to some degree depend upon, the existence of the graviton, whose existence is yet to be proven. Finally, given the aforementioned reasons no String Theory has secured wide acceptance.

Other candidate theories of everything include Loop Quantum Gravity, Superstring Theory, M-Theory and Multiverse Theory.

Loop quantum gravity (LQG) is a model that attempts to express Einstein's formulation of gravity in a quantized configuration. The theory seeks to reconcile the quantum properties of the universe and gravity. However, since its formulation there is much debate over the merits of loop quantum gravity.

Superstring theory (shorthand for supersymmetric string theory) was an attempt to treat all of the particles and fundamental forces of nature in one theory by modelling them as vibrations of infinitesimal supersymmetric strings.

M-theory was instigated by Edward Witten in 1995 to unify the five (5) versions of string theory. Scientists were troubled by the existence of numerous separate string theories. Sadly, we do not have tools to explore this theory.

The Multiverse Theory supposes that our universe is not the only one; there exist many hidden infinite possible alternate universes out there (Carr, 2009). Our universe could be just one of an infinite number of universes making up a multiverse (parallel worlds). Demonstrably, notions of parallel dimensions, alternate timelines and dimensional planes, among others, appear surreal and farfetched in the least.

Many scientists find these candidate theories of everything too speculative and most unlikely (Smolin, 2007). The reason is simple. Scientists often doubt any theory that relies on alternate and or multiple realities that we can never observe.

Debatably the dilemma scientists' face is how to reconcile general relativity (the universe on the massive scale) and quantum mechanics (the universe on the diminutive scale).

From the foregoing it is patently clear that previous efforts have not been successful. Most importantly, the lack of experimental verification may not be the main reason as to why none of these theoretical frameworks can withstand close scrutiny as the most sought theory of everything.

Connectedness successfully unites two previously incompatible fields: Einstein's formulation of gravity and quantum mechanics. Connectedness is the furthest humanity has come in efforts to unravel the Big Bang, black holes and time travel. Virtually anything can be accommodated in its expansive embrace. Besides, connectedness makes testable predictions.

CONNECTEDNESS AS THE ULTIMATE THOUGHT PROCESS

Following *The Perfect Theory: The Complete Unified Description of the Universe*, connectedness looks at the universe in terms of dimensions (Khamala, 2014a). Dimension herein refers to the property of a phenomenon[4] by which it occupies space. Physical phenomena occupy space (and have mass). Non-physical phenomena[5] neither occupy space nor have mass.

---

[4] A Phenomenon refers to any recognizable occurrence.

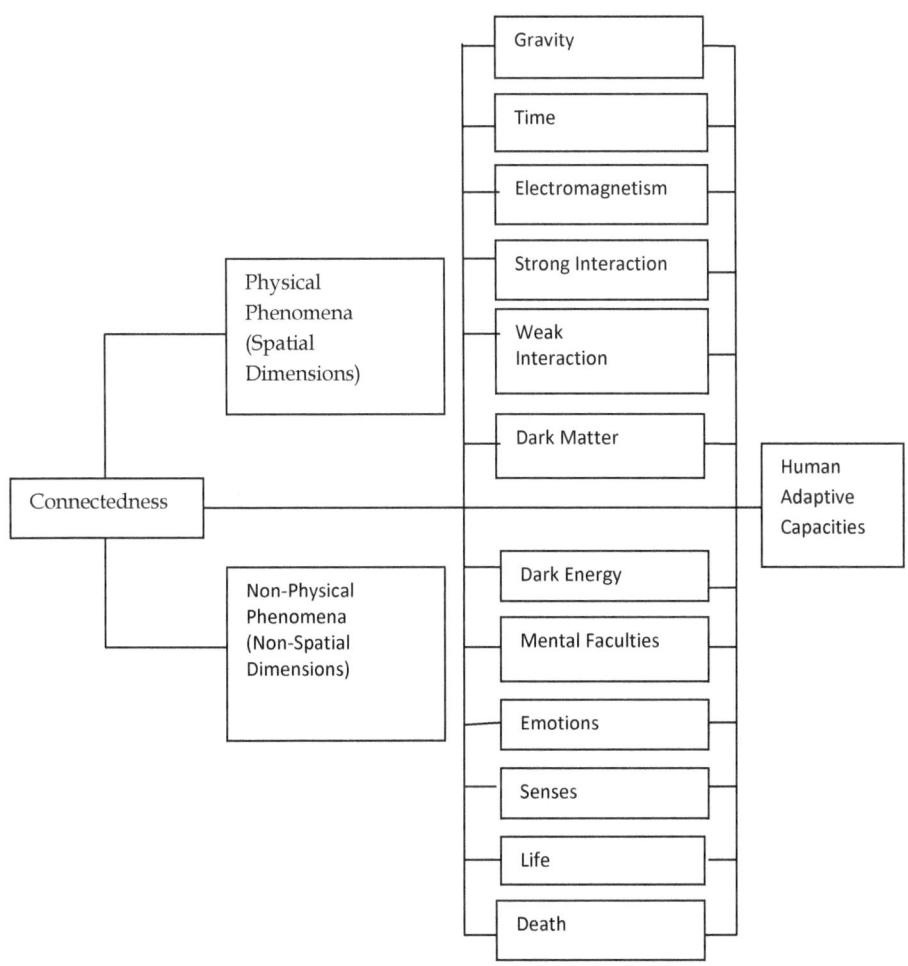

Figure 1: A Modified Illustration of Connectedness

Source: Khamala (2014a)

Connectedness effectively describes all forms of matter and the fundamental interactions. Connectedness holds that nature[6] (reality) is **spatial** (the usual way of describing the

---

natural world based on the Cartesian coordinate system), and **non-spatial dimensions**.

Spatial means any observable occurrence (phenomena) having measurable physical attributes of position (length, width and depth) and momentum. The electron, considered the smallest subatomic particle, does occupy space around nuclei, has mass and an electrical charge[7].

Following the Pauli Exclusion Principle, two electrons cannot be in the same place at the same time. However, it is basically impossible to know the exact position of an electron (and its momentum). More certainty in position equals to less uncertainty in momentum. So, electrons have particle like properties but also behave like waves. This reality correlates with the everyday observation where solid objects (physical phenomena) and have non-solid extensions.

The ultimate theoretical framework implies that besides the familiar three–dimensional physical world (space), there are twelve (12) major categories of non-spatial extensions: gravity, electromagnetism, strong nuclear interaction, weak nuclear

---

[6] Nature refers to the universe in its entirety; everything from the subatomic to the universal; animate and inanimate processes, events and behaviors.
[7] Electrons are negatively-charged particles (and protons are positively-charged while neutrons have no charge).

interaction, dark matter, dark energy, mental faculties, senses, emotions, time, life and death.

The universe is inestimable and connected as one piece but extended in non-physical realms. Things in the world tend to be distinctly one thing or the other but the universe is actually undemarcated.

According to Connectedness, a substance (solid, liquid, gas, plasma or whatever) is directly influenced both by its immediate surroundings (locality) and distant objects/events (non-locality). This view ultimately rests upon the assumption that the material universe has non-material extensions. Therefore, even when material objects are separated by large distances (potentially even trillions of light years) they are actually potentially connected in an immediate and instantaneous manner.

Framed in a different way, the physical world may stretch over the distance but retain a profound connection. This reality is best illustrated by the recent discovery of materials that make and repair themselves (e.g. self-healing synthetic polymers), the Internet, biometrics, the development of remote-controlled systems (drones), and the spread of universalist ideas such as democracy, human rights, liberty, the market, currency, the state, the incest taboo, and the family, among many others.

For quite some time, physicists have struggled to unify gravity and quantum mechanics without success. Natural scientists approach the universe (and its properties) as if it is completely removed from our existence on Earth. To complicate matters, hardly ever do social scientists (including humanities) look yonder to appreciate what natural scientists are up to however weird some of their stuff appears to be.

Connectedness uncomplicatedly fuses the understanding of the very small with that of the very large and demonstrates how this awareness intricately relates to our everyday experiences.

Connectedness raises the possibility of not only explaining natural phenomena but also political behavior, economics and social patterns.

When put this way, connectedness applies, without exception, to every important physical, chemical, atomic, molecular, biological, historical, political, economic, social and mental process in the universe.

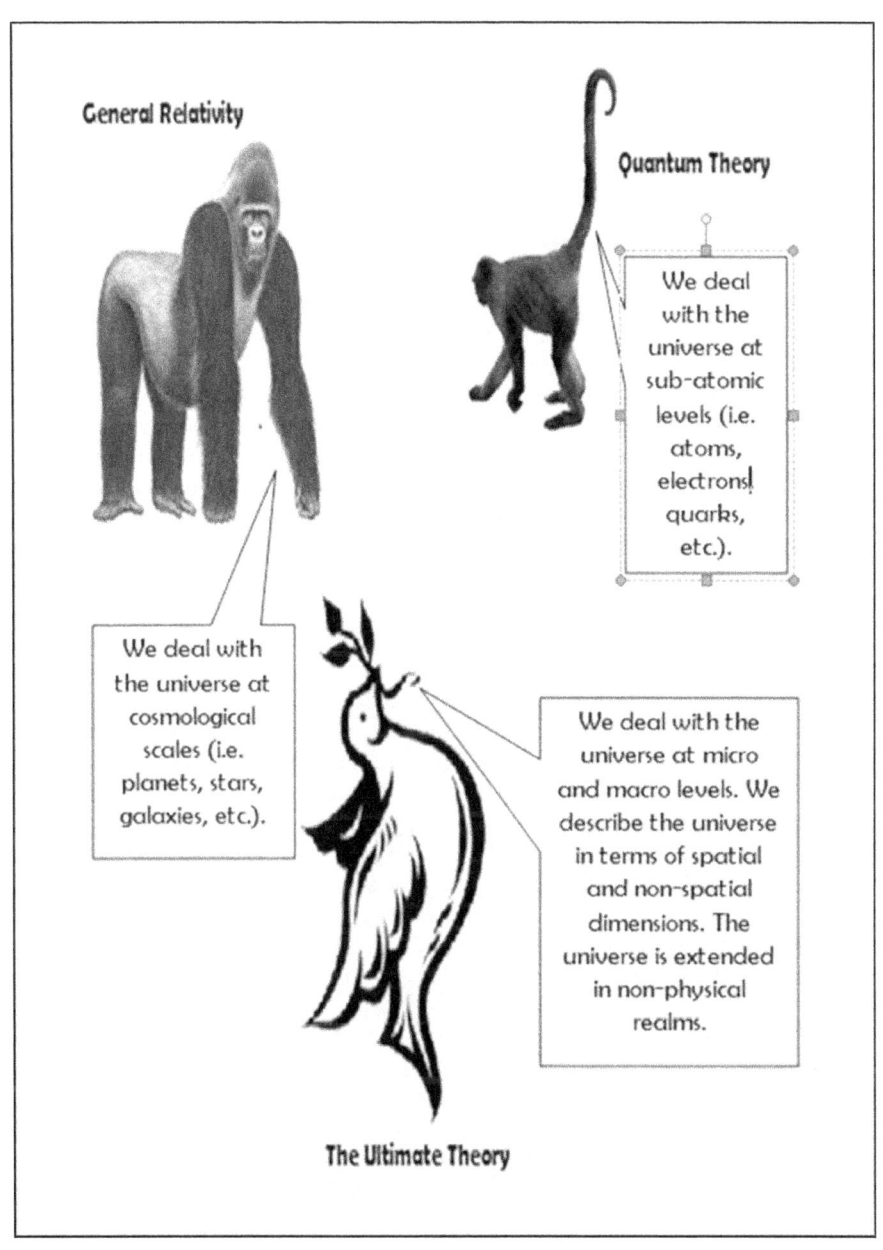

Fig 2: An Illustration of The Ultimate Theory

FUNDAMENTALS OF CONNECTEDNESS

Connectedness can be summarized as follows: the universe is described by spatial and non-spatial properties; space and its extensions cohere; change occurs at the margin; natural and social scientists study the same law(s); science is about purpose and not the method(s); and the law of nature is to sustain life.

The Universe is Spatial and Non-Spatial Relations

The universe is one wholesome piece that is extended in non-material realms. Zeno of Elea (490 – 430 BCE) confirmed that nature is integrated and never changes but its properties are isolatable and always in a flux by hypothesizing that a runner could never actually complete a race (Aristotle, 350 BCE).

Fig. 3: An Illustration of Zeno's Paradox

According to Zeno's paradox, re-interpreted in the connectedness context, in a race, the quickest runner (Achilles) can never overtake the slowest (the tortoise), since the pursuer and the pursued are one and the same. It sounds as if motion[8] is impossible. This is because for motion to occur an object must change the position which it occupies yet the universe is just about infinite but solitary (connected).

The understanding is that individual atoms acting in unison as one big particle don't behave like isolated particles. This explains why you can precisely know either the momentum of a particle or its location, but not both.

---

[8] Motion refers to movement or change in the frame of reference

The universe is singular and change (including motion) is impracticable. Each isolatable entity is a piece of the universe. Plainly put, the universe is detached but coupled by an instantaneous wholeness.

Fig. 4: Over-ground running and running on a treadmill[9]

_____

[9] A treadmill is a piece of equipment normally used for walking or running while staying in the same place.

Opposites Cohere

The universe is the way it is because of the inherent unpredictability and orderliness of its properties. The universe and its constituents cohere. Nature is intrinsically relative, random but stable. Simply put, nature is orderly. Physical components cohere with components that do not occupy space at all. Nothing and something coheres.

A vacuum is a seemingly empty spot. However, the consequence of connectedness is that no vacuum is truly empty of material objects.

There was a time when nothing became everything. The universe emerged from the precincts of nothing (the surrounding void) while life is an extension of something (the universe). Is the universe finite or infinite? There are those who subscribe to the idea that the universe had no beginning. The universe has always existed. Yet the Bing Bang theory holds that the universe was born about 13.8 billion years ago.

Electromagnetism is about the interaction of positive and negative charges (opposite values). Unlike charges attract, like ones repel. An electron has negative electric charge, and a proton has a positive charge. The attraction between them (opposite values) is what makes the electron spin around the nucleus of the atom.

Similarly, a magnet always has two poles: north and south. When pairs of magnets are tactically placed with opposite poles facing each other, they attract, whereas the same poles repel each other. The Earth is a giant magnet[10] (Pumfrey, 2002: 6). Life on our planet is because of the Earth's protective magnetic field.

Other examples of opposites that seem to cohere include physical and non-physical phenomena; matter and antimatter; visible and invisible matter; light and darkness; inside and outside; hardware and software; input and output; sleep and wakefulness; waves and particles; familiarity and strangeness; here and there; up and down; hero and antihero; heaven and hell; zero and nonzero values; gravity and weightlessness; scarcity and abundance; finite and infinity; the past and the future; and life and death; etc.

---

[10] William Gilbert (1544-1603) pioneered the idea that the Earth is a giant magnet.

Margins are Relations of Nature

Much of science is interested in understanding how things change. Change in the physical world is often the outcome of interactions at the margin. Change may or may not require bodily contact. Boundaries are relations of nature; bridges of life. Science, experience and evolution occurs at the margins.

Scientists master their environment to collapse boundaries in nature. For example, Einstein suggested that any source of mass or energy distorts (inflates, shrinks or curves) space (Einstein, 2010). A black hole, a body so massive that space closes in on itself, is an extreme example of that distortion.

Almost anything is able to become a black hole. A black hole forms when an object (e.g. a dying star) collapses under the impact of its own gravity to become a single point in space (a singularity/connectedness).

A black hole is thought of as the event horizon, the point of no return where nothing that passes through can escape (Wheeler, 2007).

The event horizon is the boundary between the black hole and the rest of the universe. Therefore, a black hole represents the margin of connectedness.

The most pertinent question that scientists have been grappling is what happens at the boundary of a black hole?

Scientists often ponder whether death can be overcome?

Nikola Tesla (1856– 1943), the famed discover of Alternative Current (AC) electric supply system, the radio and induction motor, was right on the mark when he placed premium on the study of non-physical phenomena (Seifer, 1996).

Space (the physical world) has amazing non-spatial properties. Non-spatial relations are supremely important for understanding the universe. The twelve (12) major categories of non-spatial extensions include gravity, electromagnetism, strong nuclear interaction, weak nuclear interaction, dark matter, dark energy, mental faculties, senses, emotions, time, life and death.

Gravity, for example, keeps matter together. The cosmos is the way it is because of gravity. Gravity is everywhere in the universe since it extends into space in all directions. There can be no life as we know it without gravity. Astronauts and other living organisms adjust to survive in environments characterized by microgravity (or zero gravity).

Strong nuclei and weak nuclei interactions involve atomic and molecular attractions and repulsions which act between neighboring particles (atoms, molecules or ions). The methodical study of attraction or repulsion of atomic and molecular systems (photons, electrons, ions, positrons and muons) find valuable application in our everyday life in the form of magnetic resonance, atom optics and atomic clocks (Bransden & Joachain, 2003).

Chemical reactions processes that involve the attraction and repulsion of charges are governed by electromagnetism (Pollack & Stump, 2001). Atoms either lose or gain an outer electron and thus exhibit a net positive charge or gain a net negative charge. Since the electron is negative, when an atom gains electrons in its outer shell it gains a negative charge whereas when it loses electrons it gains a positive (protons) charge. Non-conductors block electrical charge. Conductors transfer electric charge with ease. Electromagnetism finds application in our everyday lives in the form of the battery, magnet and electricity. The Earth is a massive magnet.

Scientists suggest that we have the visible universe (normal matter) and the invisible universe (dark matter and dark energy) (Nicolson, 2007; Panek, 2011). The visible universe is made of protons, neutrons, and electrons that collectively constitute atoms. NASA's Wilkinson Microwave Anisotropy Probe (WMAP) and the Planck spacecraft observations of the Cosmic Microwave Background (CMB) suggest that normal matter represents roughly a paltry 5% of the universe. Dark matter makes up about 25% while dark energy constitutes roughly 70% of the universe.

The Hubble Space Telescope (HST) observations of very distant supernovae in 1998 demonstrated that the universe is actually expanding faster than it did in the past. However, given the standard expectation would be that the expansion of the universe would be slowing not accelerating. Scientists attribute this accelerating expansion of the universe to dark energy. The arguments goes that more space routinely come into existence. Empty space is not nothing however. So, as more space comes into existence, dark energy repels gravity and causes the universe to expand faster and faster.

Connectedness applies at subatomic levels and on the scale of the entire universe. According to connectedness, dark matter and dark energy are non-spatial properties of the physical world. Dark matter and dark energy are the invisible phenomena that occupy the vast reaches of space. Dark matter and dark energy are of interest to humans because they provide a clue on the composition, evolution and ultimate fate of the universe.

Senses are the primary way of interacting with the outside world. Sense perception enables us to gain knowledge about the world.

Time is another important non-spatial dimension of the universe. Intuitively time flows in only one direction: from past to future. Actually, the dimension of time is essentially one of the properties of the natural world. Time is a non-spatial dimension dealing with the concept of duration. Time is the mental makeup that facilitates the sequencing and comparison of experienced (physical) events. Motion refers to a change in spatial position [*sic*] as the time coordinate is varied. Time is traversable in either direction. Time is neutral – it is not circular, wave, spiral, sinusoidal or linear. Time is simultaneous. The past, the present and the future are merely comparative.

Human life-forms have always desired to witness the past, present and future simultaneously. The human quest for the capacity to glimpse the beginning of time and predict the future manifests in diverse crafts such as magic, witchcraft, alchemy, astrology, prophecy, religion and present-day science. When scientists imagine faster-than-light travel, it is indicative of the human desire to overcome the limitation of mortal life (time) (Khamala, 2009; 2014a; 2014b; 2014c).

Life and death are important non-spatial relations of the natural world. Life begins at the margin of the universe during conception (or when a sperm unites with an oocyte during fertilization). The universe itself arises from the margins of seemingly empty space. Similarly, death occurs at the margins of the universe when the property of life is lost. Nonetheless, gametes link generations a clear indication that life is a continuum. Following demise, the remains of an organism become part of the biogeochemical cycle process to fashion other substances and life forms.

Indeed, a popular Buddhist excerpt observes that when birds are alive, they devour ants. When birds pass on, ants devour them.

Some say death is finality. We are destined to die without exception. Nothing lasts forever. Actually, death is not our destiny. Everything lasts forever.

Same Law(s) Govern Natural Phenomena, Human Behavior and Social Patterns

Science is a cooperative venture. Knowledge lies at the boundary of natural (natural/physical sciences) and human-made (humanities/social sciences) phenomena. However, the interface of natural sciences and humanities and social sciences remain largely unexplored.

Think of it, human interactions and relations determine what use technologies are put to. Flying machines, for example, were initially mere science fiction. They then became reality in the airplane. Later, they were adapted for war. Lately, drone attacks and surveillance have become a common occurrence for surveillance purpose and as weaponry.

To understand why inventions and innovations end up being used to fuel and drive competition, division and conflict it is important to understand non-spatial relations such as mental faculties (conceptualization of power, justice, hegemony, imperialism, freedom, democracy, scarcity, etc.) emotions (anger, fear, etc.), life and death.

Science is an Adaptive Capacity

Science is more than the scientific method - scholarly dialogue and validation of results. Science as an adaptive capacity, which encompasses evolution, experience, academic engagements and technology, is purpose-driven and value-laden. Science is the practical and intellectual adaptive activity capacity to preserve life endlessly in the long term by collapsing boundaries through the discovery of the underlying rhythm of the universe.

Non-spatial relations (phenomena) are the subject of scientific inquiry, experience and evolution. Kant underscored this reality in the form of 'the-thing-in-itself' viz-as-viz phenomena (Kant, 1848).

Science is premised on the awareness that the universe is predictable and follows a set of discoverable rules. For some people, child play involves repetitive, routine, random and useless activities that children participate in to pass time.

Actually, child play (and development) is a form of science (maturation and learning). For humans to evolve an upright posture, for example, they had to overcome gravity. Mastery of bipedalism is acquired and perfected through child play.

As people age, they become frail and inexorably lose control of their non-spatial properties that include electromagnetism, gravity, senses, mental faculties, emotions and in due course life.

Karl Groos in *The Play of Animals* (1898) and *The Play of Man* (1901) demonstrated that sports and recreation enables animals and humans to put into practice the skills, knowledge and expertise they need to survive and reproduce.

The Dictum of the Universe is to Preserve Life

Boundaries are edges of knowledge and understanding. The most distinctive boundary is that which separates life and death.

Living and inanimate things occupy space and are extended in non-physical realms. Whereas advanced life forms emerged from simpler organisms, the first living organisms emerged from inanimate matter. What differentiates animate from inanimate is the property of life.

Scientists have failed for centuries to succinctly define life (Schrödinger, 2012). Defining life is understandably difficult because life does not actually exist in the physical sense. Life is a non-spatial dimension of nature.

Life and death are vital characteristics of the universe such that an entity is inanimate, dying or animate. Life and death are opposites.

Death occurs when the property of life is lost. So, what is death exactly? Well, scientists are yet to give a lucid, concise and comprehensive definition of death. Actually, like life, death is a non-spatial property of nature.

Death is perhaps one of science's biggest mysteries. Death also happens to be the most important problem in science. Bereavement causes pain and sorrow. Mourning is the human expression of frustration with death. People shout, cry, wail, maim, kill and even die in reaction to death.

Experience, evolution and science are attempts to overcome death. New scientific approaches, medications, cures, techniques, inventions, coding of life, the development of complex technologies and the whole scientific edifice is about how to postpone and or halt the dying process.

Death touches every phase of human experience.

Relatedness was originally meant to collapse the borderline between life and death. The incest taboo, which is almost universal and that has a biological basis, besides preventing the health setbacks associated with inbreeding, it also helps to avoid competition and conflict that may lead to premature death within the family. The survival of the family and current social organization and patterns rests on the restriction of sex among its members and the consequent need for other family units as sources of spouses. The incest taboo normally extends to close (and sometimes distant) relatives for the same purpose thus bringing into its fold family lines, lineages and exogamic clans.

Whereas the kinship principle has for the most part been fundamental to social organization, the grouping of individuals of different family lines and lineages into age-sets, age-grades and other loyalties worked to ease divisiveness that is a recipe for premature demise.

The family and the successive socio-political identities are therefore adaptive capacities to extend life and sidestep bereavement.

Unluckily, human socio-political and economic institutions (i.e. families, lineages, clans, castes, ethnicities, nation-states, races, religions, and/or civilizations) simply solidify human groups, deflect and externalize competition, conflict and death.

Manifestly, almost all sub-optimal outcomes such as wars, the holocaust, genocide, ethnic cleansing, apartheid, extermination, enforced disappearance of persons, persecution, forcible transfer of populations, economic fluctuations, unemployment, poverty and the rise and disintegration of successive civilizations correlate with botched attempts to establish, maintain or dismantle unequal power relations (or hegemonies).

Relatedness constrains resources and is a barrier to the development of complex technologies to sustain life. Relatedness is responsible for imperialism in all its manifestations (slavery, colonialism and neo-colonialism). Globalization, the newest variety of imperialism, is simply externalization of competition, enmity and death. Globalization thrives on power as an end, economic exclusion, exploding inequality and the obsession with money.

Connectedness offers an alternative way of organizing society instead of human restricted enclaves based on relatedness.

Connectedness (unlike globalization) necessitates toning down on competition, greed and selfishness along fault lines. Connectedness is anchored on a clear demonstrable common goal or value system. Connectedness can prevent the world from being nuclearized, stem injudicious competition and conflicts and the trauma of war. Connectedness is, therefore, a unique way of confronting unknowns (e.g. death) that require huge collaborations with people from all over the world.

There are so many ways to oblivion of life as we know it. Humans study phenomena to discover how to survive basically anything: natural disasters, crippling pressure, lack of oxygen, extreme temperatures, radiation, dehydration, darkness, predation, disease, the aging process, and perilous competition in the world society, among other extremes.

The hermit crab and a number of microscopic freshwater animals can live for centuries. So far only the jellyfish *turritopsis nutricula* is effectively immortal (Piraino *et al.*, 1996). The jellyfish can indefinitely alternate between its adult form and its infantile stage.

Death has always been central to people's lives. According to connectedness, immortality is not just possible, but plausible, or even probable.

CONCLUSION

This chapter has reviewed previous theorization of the natural world and rendered connectedness as the ultimate explanation of the universe. The emphasis of the perfect abstraction is on the relationship between space and non-spatial dimensions. Twelve (12) non-spatial properties were elaborated namely gravity, electromagnetism, strong nuclear interaction, weak nuclear interaction, dark matter, dark energy, mental faculties, senses, emotions, time, life and death.

CHAPTER THREE

CONNECTEDNESS IN THE REAL WORLD

INTRODUCTION

Connectedness explains how everything in the world is inter-related. Our uncritical view of the universe is one characterized by demarcations, interludes and unfilled intervals. In reality, the universe is one wholesome thing that is extended in non-physical realms. Connectedness is about contact along the margins. Contact may or may not necessarily be physical.

GEOGRAPHICAL CONNECTEDNESS

Throughout history, geography has significantly influenced human contact. Previously, geography necessitated that human beings organize themselves into definite groups based solely on birth (relatedness). That being the case, for thousands of years our ancestors lived in small and isolated populations.

Through airways, railways, roadways, laneways, runways, waterways and dataways humans have managed to exploit the benefits and limitations presented by geography. There are no geographical and time barriers any more. The Internet, for example, enables people to interact on social media, communicate, collaborate and share information even when they are miles away from each other.

Centuries before the Sahara became a desert, trans-Saharan trade, intermarriages, knowledge sharing and exchange made it possible to people to interact with their environment to continue life (Ki-Zerbo, 1990; Mazrui, 1999; Ogot, 1999; Sharman, 2013). Climatic changes between 5000 and 1500 BCE produced the Sahara Desert limiting human contact and other positive interactions. After the Sahara became arid, the gulf between North Africa and sub-Saharan Africa became apparent.

Pan-Africanism emerged in the nineteenth century to facilitate recognition and solidarity among people of African descent both on the continent and in the Diaspora (Walters, 1993; Esedebe, 1994 & Ackah, 1999; Mazrui, 1999). During this early phase, the emphasis of this Afrocentric narrative was on the place of Africans and Africa's contribution to the development of human civilization.

Prominent pan-Africanists include Olaudah Equiano, Ottobah Cugoano, Edward Wilmot Blyden, Fredrick Douglass, JE

Casely Hayford, Martin Robinson Delany, Henry Sylvester Williams, Malcolm X, Marcus Garvey, George Padmore, Isaac Wallace-Johnson, Frantz Fanon, Aimé Césaire, Paul Robeson, CLR James, WEB Du Bois, Walter Rodney, Léopold Sédar Senghor, Cheikh Anta Diop, Ladipo Solanke, Kwame Nkrumah, Sékou Ahmed Touré, Ahmed Ben Bella, Julius Nyerere, Jomo Kenyatta, Amilcar Cabral, Patrice Lumumba and Muammar Gaddafi.

Pan-Africanism (a form of relatedness) is now dated. Eurocentricism and Afrocentrism are two sides of the same coin. Connectedness is the appropriate pathway for sustainable continental unity.

Today connectedness enthusiasts prefer a continent-based approach, which considers Africa as a whole with emphasis on historical and contemporary connections with other continents. In pursuit of this aspiration, Internet giants such as Google and Facebook, plans to deliver and expand wireless internet connectivity in Africa and other continents.

For centuries, humans have measured and mapped out worldly phenomena. Humans from early on primarily relied on a built-in GPS system to remember routes but they also used physical landmarks that are well-known to deliver accurate location information. Today, the latitude and longitude grid (or datum) is pegged to a model of the planet's shape (Musser, 2013).

The Global Positioning System (GPS) came about when Einstein sought to correct logical inconsistencies in the Newtonian universe. GPS is a space-based satellite navigation system that provides position, navigation and time information to users worldwide in all weather conditions on or near the Earth's surface (El-Rabbany, 2002).

The Earth's surface is always in a flux, and as such, no object on its surface has predetermined coordinates (address). GPS satellites are programmed to account for the effects of relativity.

Spatial thinking, especially the use of mapping technology (e.g. Google Maps), can be a remarkably powerful tool for understanding the workings of connectedness. Connectedness is redrawing the map of the world. Only few remote locations do not have officially documented geographical coordinates.

PHYSICAL CONNECTEDNESS

The universe is one wholesome thing constituted by physical and non-physical components. Corporeal components of the universe incorporate anything that has mass, takes up space and that can be seen or felt. Yet material objects are not distinct from their non-physical properties. Material entities and their properties interact with the environment. Spatial connectedness occurs whenever an object or environment changes.

Physical objects are revealed to us through senses. Senses are perceptual capacities of the brain that enable human beings to represent and understand the milieu.

Senses in human beings comprise those that perceive external stimuli; those that perceive the body's own position, motion, and state; and those that perceive sensations in internal organs such as pain and balance. External senses include sound, sight, touch, smell, taste, temperature differences and direction. Perception of the surroundings can be shaped by learning, memory, and expectation. Physical connectedness (senses) facilitates experience. Experience (as in walking, talking, sleeping, yawning, playing, thinking, etc.) is the attempt to avoid premature death.

Physical familiarity (physical attractions and sexual urges) determines human behavior, social patterns and human interaction with their environment. Trying to manage sexual expression has been an enduring dilemma since the beginning of organized society. Sigmund Freud emphasized the centrality of the sexual life in human development (Freud, 2001).

Think of it, the survival of the family rests on the restriction of sex among its members and the consequent need for other family units as sources of spouses (Khamala, 2009; 2014a; 2014b). Marriage and or sexual relations involving a person's close relatives are prohibited by the incest taboo.

The actual motivations underlying revealing fashion is to increase contact (but not necessarily physical). Human beings desire to bond with fellow human beings.

Our very existence restricts our traits and behavior. Human relationships are the way they are (public, private and personal spaces) because of taboos, norms, customs, long-held traditions, regulations, laws and constitutional frameworks.

EMOTIONAL CONNECTEDNESS

Emotional connectedness is the individual's trait levels of feeling that manifest as they interact with their surroundings. Basic emotions include love, happiness, compassion, empathy, nurturance, altruism, fear, sadness, mourning, anger, aggression and disgust. Emotional sensation is associated with mood, temperament, personality, disposition, and motivation.

Emotion is an integral property of nature; one of the twelve (12) non-spatial dimensions of nature. Activities such as music, literature, art, scenic beauty and love mimics nature and as such heighten nostalgic emotions. Essentially, during nostalgic moments humans are able to unify the experienced life (mortal life) with the desired life (infinity).

The hunt for love is a human preoccupation that has puzzled us for centuries. Why do humans fall in or out of love? Opposite-sex friendships contribute to individual and collective well-being. Why do we empathize with others? Evidence abound showing that we automatically take on others' facial expressions, postures, moods, and even patterns of brain activity (de Waal, 2008). In essence, we experience this person's state as our own.

Negative global spectacles such as major wars (WW1, WW2 and the Cold War), genocide and terrorism are associated with widespread discontent, insecurity and hopelessness. The greatest contentment is found in positive social interactions and relationships.

Generally, human beings prioritize those pursuits that enable them to experience positive emotions and feel a sense of purpose. A sense of purpose is an orientation to something bigger than the self (and the selfless). People need meaning to thrive. The key to a meaningful life is serving society and enabling others to find their function in life.

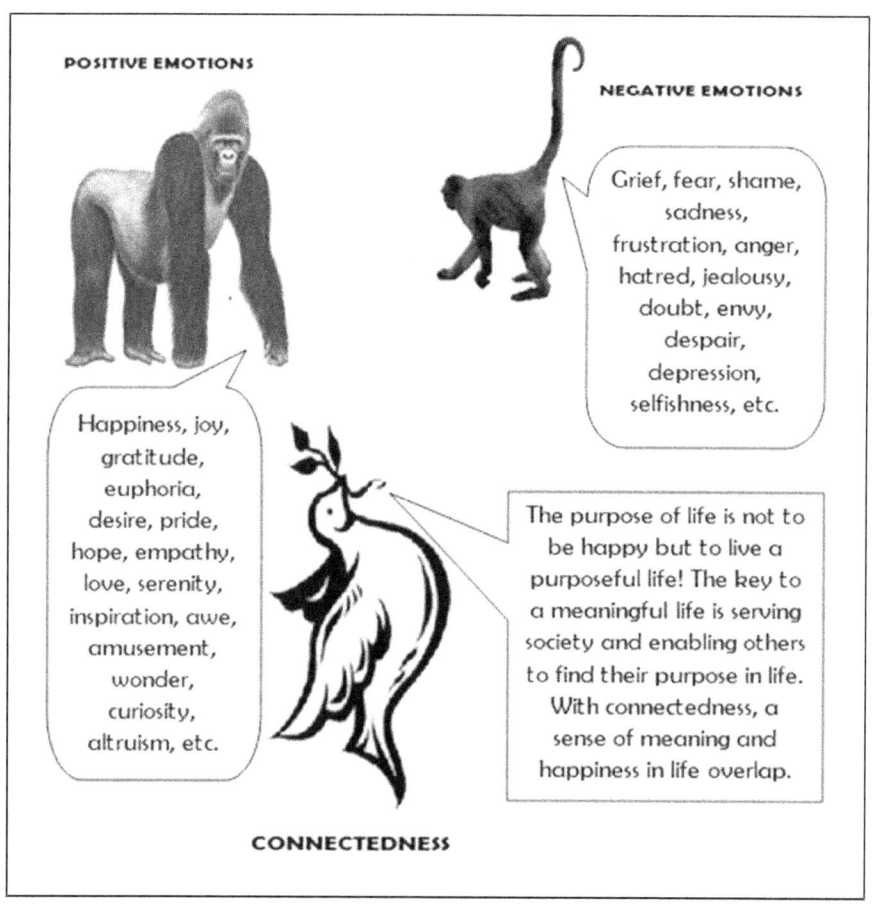

Fig. 5: The Meaning of Life

Connectedness summarizes purpose-driven happiness. With connectedness, a sense of meaning and happiness in life have common characteristics.

SOCIAL CONNECTEDNESS

Why do people play football or any other sport activity for that matter? Of course some people are not fans of games. But why do people who never play games care about sports events anyway? In fact, sometimes spectators seem to enjoy the game more than the players themselves! Why?

Sports and other pastimes are avenues for social (and emotional) connectedness. Global sporting events like the World Cup and the Olympics give humanity a chance to connect.

Social connectedness refers to a person's interactions with others and the benefits these positive social interactions and relationships can bring to the individual as well as to society (Spellerberg, 2001).

Social connectedness takes the form of social support (i.e. empathy, praise, attention, and generosity); attachment; sense of belonging; and sense of being familiar with somebody.

The quality of social connectedness is determined by the duration of relationship; frequency of interaction; knowledge of each other's intent; physical intimacy or closeness; self-disclosure; social circle network familiarity; and exclusiveness.

Social interactions can occur at individual level (self); school level (school and teachers; family level (parents and siblings); kin level (related by family ties); intimate level (friends and romantic partners); peers level; professional level (fellowships, membership to professional associations); neighborhoods level; ideological level (religion, political party); and many other levels.

The level and quality of social connectedness as in closeness and distance in same-sex and opposite-sex relationships help define friends, strangers and even enemies. Some social practices reinforce friendship and other ties for example the handshake, sports, etc. Some social practices encourage exclusiveness, discrimination and enmity such as nepotism, clannism, tribalism, racism and religious intolerance. Xenophobia denotes unreasonable fear or hatred of foreigners or strangers.

Humans have brief interactions or long term interactions in the form of marriage. The ancestral condition for humans is probably living in pairs to stem competition for mating partners and to facilitate parental care. Therefore, marriage, whether monogamous or polygamous, evolved as a mating strategy to sustain life.

Whereas pairbonding (monogamy) appears to be the trademark of human reproductive strategy, unfaithfulness is not that infrequent. Notwithstanding the near universal condemnation of infidelity, this behavior occurs worldwide with astonishing regularity. Why? Infidelity is also nature's way of sustaining life!

Human beings come together to celebrate milestones in their lives such as birthdays, weddings, anniversaries. Social events come in handy in the process of maintaining relationships and networks.

Human life is depended on rituals, narratives and shared practices that create and sustain the social bond. Marriage, for example, is a union in which peace is cemented and celebrated.

Humans participate in collective rites of bidding farewell as a way of reconciling with loss collectively.

Scientists have long sought insights into how we perceive the world and what motivates our behavior. Social situations can affect human behavior. People respond to social influence. Relatedness inclines humans to be intolerant, unkind and wicked to tribal others but connectedness inculcates in us the propensity to be empathetic, kind and good to other fellow humans.

Much of the current world crisis comes down to a battle of identities. People (lacking long-term shared goals) have been socialized to identity less and less as wholes and more and more as separate groups (relatedness). The cure is to encourage people to see themselves as one whole.

Nothing is solitary. Even humans are social, and therefore, ill-equipped to live in isolation. This explains why humans live in family groups, form professional clubs or even complex organizations such as NGOs, companies and states.

Lately, the internet and social media sites such as Facebook, Twitter, Weibo (China's equivalent of Twitter), Google+, You Tube and Instagram are making it possible for millions of users globally to interact and share experiences day after day.

LinkedIn is facilitating professionals to network on an international scale for job placements, sales prospects or just to share experience.

Social networks compliment traditional forms of meeting and socializing. In view of this, social connectedness is becoming a reality every day.

Social connectedness is about individual and societal progress and development. Success (individual and collective) is often the outcome of a combination of individual effort, fate, luck and the goodwill of others. However, human intervention and mastery of hard work and the goodwill of others to a large extent determine chance (fate and luck). It is upon humanity to create suitable environments for people to leave positive marks on the world.

GENDER CONNECTEDNESS

Men and women are defined by their biological and physiological characteristics. Sex divisions do not vary significantly across the world. Underpinning the definition of sex as a category is the purpose of being man or woman which is to continue life. Masculine and feminine divisions are socially constructed gender categories. Gender divisions vary significantly across different human societies. Gender aspects and stereotyping breeds relatedness. Without gender divisions and prejudice there would be no relatedness.

Identity formation occurs though the subordination and domination of either gender (Khamala, 2009; 2014a). When individuals or groups of individuals are labeled as different, structures of divisions and disunity are created in the society where gender is the organizing concept. Remarkable gender structured power units include families (the inheritance of surnames), lineages, clans, castes, ethnicities, nation-states, races, religions, and civilizations.

Identity construction and reproduction breeds struggles within and between constructed identities with either gender (mostly men) projecting the strength of the group through competition and different manifestations of imperialism such as slavery, colonialism, terrorism, conflicts, war and genocide.

In most cultures men are expected to be strong, brave and willing to protect themselves and their families (masculinity) while women are expected to be loyal and chaste (femininity). Men's propensity for risk-taking as reinforced by gender norms explain why human males and females differ so markedly in their average longevity.

Historical reality and worldwide trends indicate that the scope for force in world affairs is narrowing. Social behaviours that perpetuate or celebrate violence premised on appropriate' behaviour of men and women as dictated by society are slowly being discarded. The recent integration of women in combat roles to aid the war effort has not helped. The question becomes why? Gendered power units are constructed and reproduced because of the unequal relationships between men and women. Gender equality collapses divisions rendering discrimination, competition, violence and force unnecessary.

Connectedness is the realization that all human beings belong to a single world community.

BIOLOGICAL CONNECTEDNESS

Relatedness is the key concept in the study of life. Biology essentially deals with organisms' genetics (gene relatedness), their roles in their ecosystems, and with whom they can mate. In actuality, we are all related if you go far enough back. One is connected to previous and future generations through Deoxyribonucleic Acid (DNA).

Charles Darwin[11] (1809 - 1882) suggested that life-forms adapt and evolve gradually to survive (Darwin, 1859). Later, Richard Dawkins formulated a gene-centred version of this theory and suggested that it is genes that adapt and evolve to survive, not individual organisms or groups (Dawkins, 1976). So, the individual gene dubbed 'the selfish gene' just uses the individual organism as a vehicle to propagate itself.

Darwin's theory and even Dawkin's variant theory of evolution are based on self-interest and self-preservation. But cooperation, common in real life, was a puzzle to Darwin. He was particularly struck by social insects especially their ability to work together and cooperate when tackling tasks (Wilson, 1971).

Evidence seems to indicate that natural selection does not favour individuals or groups that are exploitative and selfish (Nilesh *et al.*, 2012). Selfish people and groups eventually contend each other out of existence. Predictably, collective

---

[11] Charles Darwin did not think up the phrase "survival of the fittest." This expression was in fact first used by Herbert Spencer in his 1864 *Principles of Biology*. In later editions, Darwin found the phrase expedient.

preservation dictates that collective interests come before self-interest.

Genetic diversity is nature's mechanism to deal with relatedness and premature demise. Sexual reproduction ensures genetic diversity. Sex allows two organisms to shuffle their genes, creating better adapted offspring. Unrelated partners of the same species contribute half of their DNA to form a unique fertile offspring. Genetic diversity enables species to become stronger, avoid inherited diseases and better able to adapt to change. Evolution is the change in the genetic makeup of a population over time. Species diversity is nature's way of increasing the chances of sustaining life in the universe.

Death is the most important challenge that confronts biological life. Grieving is often a period of self-reflection. Mourning is not entirely selfless, however. Mourning is humanity's preferred mode of affirming collective preservation.

Early on when humans were at the mercy of nature death was seen as the will of the gods until the discovery of the causes, symptoms and treatment of diseases. Nowadays natural calamities such as floods, drought, famine, and many others are no longer considered inevitable and deadly thanks to contemporary science.

Biomedical research, vaccines, curative successes, diet, bipedality, clothing and the search of extraterrestrial life represent ongoing adaptations to overcome disease, climate and terrain to save lives.

TECHNOLOGICAL CONNECTEDNESS

Technology is an attempt to imitate and control nature to sustain life. Humans exploit their natural instincts and immediate environment to survive and progress. Humanity is venerated for technological ingenuity. Nevertheless, technology without recourse to human values or ideas of morality is unsafe.

Many scientists have been greatly disappointment when their adaptations have been deployed to resolve unjustified terrestrial squabbles.

Mikhail Kalashnikov, the inventor of AK-47, was disturbed that the weapon he designed for defense purposes was the weapon of choice in the murder millions of people around the world (Chivers, 2013). Kalashnikov, a tank commander, designed the AK 47 assault rifle for defense purposes when his country, then the USSR, was battling the Germans during World War II. Today the AK 47 rifle is the weapon of choice in military conflicts, coup d'états, genocides, identity skirmishes and criminal operations.

Julius Robert Oppenheimer (1904 – 1967) is most remembered as the 'father of the atomic bomb' for his role (together with Enrico Fermi) in the World War II Manhattan Project that developed the first nuclear weapons (Monk, 2013). However, after the atomic bombings of Hiroshima and Nagasaki, Oppenheimer was concerned of the possibility of nuclear weapons being unleashed against civilian targets resulting in millions of deaths.

Oppenheimer's resistance the use of his innovation to maim and kill contributed to his isolation, frustration and humiliation. He was in due course suspected of being an agent of the Soviet Union and hurled before Senator McCarthy's infamous House Un-American Activities Committee in 1954.

From thereon, Oppenheimer persistently underscored the complicatedness of harnessing the benefits of scientific knowledge in a world in which the freedom to exchange ideas is curtailed by political concerns.

Kalashnikov and Oppenheimer's experiences symbolize the moral dilemma many scientists face when they realize they can't control how others would use their research in a universe characterized by relatedness.

Relatedness limits the benefits of technology and help recruit talented scientists to engage in unproductive ventures such as assault, murder and war.

The dangers of mixing technology with relatedness are clear. Competition and rivalry encourages research investments for defensive and aggression purposes. Demonstrably, throughout history, humans have invested so much energy in building destructive technologies such as the nuclear bomb, biological, chemical weapons, cyber-terrorism and other newer forms of warfare. Today we are witnessing the gradual militarization of drones.

Technology has frequently been driven by the military before being deployed for civilian use as an afterthought. For instance, today space missions are more about global stature than about technical expertise to solve deep human problems.

Alfred Nobel (1833–1896) invented dynamite (Fant, 1996; Nobelprize.org, 2014). Whereas he thought his invention would end all wars, to many it was seen as a lethal weapon of choice in war.

A story is told that when his brother Ludvig died while visiting Cannes in France, a French newspaper mistakenly ran Alfred's obituary headlined, "The merchant of death is dead".

Following this event, a concerned and disappointed Alfred Nobel decided to leave a better legacy after his death. He was not satisfied to be remembered merely as an armaments manufacturer who contributed to the demise of millions of people.

Wanting to go down in history with a more positive epitaph, he opted to reward people whose work helps humanity by establishing the now famous Nobel Prizes. In his will, he allocated a substantial part of his total assets to establish the five Nobel Prizes to honour outstanding achievers yearly for strides made in subjects that interested him, namely Physics, Chemistry, Medicine, Literature, and Peace. An Economics Prize was added later.

Connectedness (unlike globalization) necessitates toning down on competition, greed and selfishness along fault lines. Connectedness reasserts the veracity that the scientific enterprise is consultative, collaborative and life-affirming.

While immortality may not be a reality yet, rapidly evolving technology is making it more realistic.

LEGAL CONNECTEDNESS

History is replete with horrendous atrocities committed against humankind. Human societies since olden times have set up justice structures to redress human suffering and injustice. Mention can be made of pre-Biblical laws (commonly described as an 'eye for an eye' system of justice) particularly Ur-Nammu of the city of Ur, the Sumerian Code of Lipit-Ishtar of Isin and the laws of Hammurabi. Today, the ICC is a global court of last resort. The ICC adjudicates crimes against humanity.

The trend all over the world is that people don't want governments to violate their personal space except when trying to prevent or deter rape and other sexual violations. People also want governments to play their regulatory and oversight functions in their economic life within defined parameters. People also don't want their governments to use public resources to prop repressive regimes, undertake imprudent surveillance undertakings, sabotage the world economy or threaten world peace.

Legal connectedness represents our commitment to the sanctity of life, human dignity, justice, constitutionalism, human freedom and universal ideals.

SPIRITUAL CONNECTEDNESS

Religion is closely intertwined with scholarship starting with early speculation on the nature of the universe (Khamala, 2014c). Early on, religious entrepreneurs discovered that to avoid bereavement one requires unusual might. It is this realization that bore notions of supernatural forces, deities, gods, and God. Since then religion has been a part of daily life for many people around the world. The belief in occult and clairvoyant sciences still persists to this day.

Many religions are usually ethno-specific and therefore inseparable from relatedness. Predictably, most religions have had a dynamic and turbulent history. Unlike most religions, Christianity and Islam have been characterized by a connectedness influence. Jesus Christ and Mohammad were exceptional trying to triumph over relatedness. Christianity and Islam opened a universal worldview.

Universalist religion has made commerce, travel and human interaction on a world scale possible. Religion has helped built schools, roads, hospitals, provide electricity and water and nurture entrepreneurs in many parts of the world.

Not everything about religion is rosy however.

The misuse of religion has a long and bizarre history. Brutal kings in the Middle Ages invoked the name of God to justify their immoral rulership (Bauer, 2010).

Nowadays, wanton killing and aimless violence associated with global terrorism clouds the core message of religious conviction that stresses the sanctity of human life and prescribe a path of non-violence, tolerance and peace.

Many people associate religion with fanaticism, fundamentalism, intolerance, superstition and ignorance. Communism under Joseph Stalin, Pol Pot and Mao Zedong banned religion altogether. And much of the conflict in the world is often blamed on religion.

But why does religion persist?

Religion endures because it sheds light on some of the basic questions of existence, gives meaning to life and raises the prospect of reincarnation, resurrection and eternal life.

Science and religion are just different styles of approaching the same problem. In other words, religion is a reminder that humanity is yet to solve the problem of science, which is death. Death is the ultimate loss for it dispossesses us of experiences, milestones and possibilities.

Religious entrepreneurs hope to collapse the border between life and death.

Jesus (7 BCE – 30 CE), the central figure of Christianity, imagined the possibility of life after death. Jesus' resurrection[12] is fundamental to the Christian faith. Resurrection is a common motif in Abrahamic and non-Abrahamic faiths.

Even physicists, mathematicians and other mainstream scientists have pondered over the possibility of some physical form of hereafter (Tipler, 1997).

GLOBAL POLITICAL CONNECTEDNESS

Power is the key concept in political science. Power is synergetic. Power is not an end in itself rather it is a means to sustain life.

---

[12] Resurrection refers to the act of coming back to life after having died.

Power as intrigues, drama and intense behind-the-scenes lobbying is relatedness. Power as informed by relatedness often fails to advance the interests of society as a whole.

Popular works such as Robert Green's *The 48 Laws of Power* (1998) and Niccollo Machiavelli's *The Prince* (1532) are now contextualized. Their portrayal of raw power does not sit well with contemporary connectedness set-ups. Connectedness encourages participation, consultation, consensus-building and agenda-setting.

Synergetic power revolves around the individual leader, institutions and an overriding cause. Synergetic leadership enlists the support and participation necessary to accomplish the will of the universe.

Politics largely deals with participation and representation in decision-making in the process of the allocation of value. Politics has a domestic and international dimension. Demonstrably amoral politics is out of sync with the edict of the universe. Those who use power wisely are venerated throughout the ages as moral icons while who abuse power receive contemptuous treatment.

Leaders such as Alexander the Great ((356 – 323 BCE, King of Macedonia); Julius Caesar (100 – 44 BCE, extended the Roman

Empire to its furthest limits); Napoleon (1769 – 1821, emperor of France); and Adolf Hitler (1889 – 1945, *Fuehrer* of Nazi Germany), tried but failed to conquer the world.

The truly inspirational historical leaders on the scale of Nelson Mandela (1918-2013) sacrificed their own happiness for the common good.

Of late, democracy is the preferred political system in the world. Apparently, liberal democracy (as in representative democracy) is emerging as the most predominant variant of democracy (Fukuyama, 1992). However, one of the biggest challenges that confront political liberalism is how to deal with relatedness.

Liberal political theory takes relatedness (competition, division, nationalism, etc.) as given truths. Given relatedness, political loyalties reflect ethnic (or other related identity) differences instead of ideological and political clarity. Many times people end up being mobilized along lines of relatedness with political parties acting as smokescreens of underlying divisions, tensions and hatreds. The end result of partisan politics is that members of named human socio-political and economic institutions pin their hopes on identity entrepreneurs and rally behind them relegating the bigger picture.

Stereotyping of people based on relatedness often lead people to draw unfair and potentially damaging conclusions about entire populations. Group identity premised on physical appearance (nose, eye color, skin pigmentation, or hair) or any other phenotypical criteria is the path to damnation and this clearly manifests in different forms of corruption such as clannism, nepotism, tribalism, cronyism, racism, religious extremism, international belligerence, and other forms of exclusivisms.

Some of the undesirable outcomes of relatedness include clan warfare, tribal clashes, genocide, refugees, sectarian conflicts, civilizational collapse, assorted shapes of imperialism, global terrorism and war.

When the Soviet Union collapsed and the Cold War ended, Fukuyama fundamentally misread these events as the ideological triumph of liberal capitalist democracy over Soviet communism. He was not alone. Fukuyama and those who share his school of thought failed to decipher the discomforting truth that geopolitics is actually relatedness. This became apparent when in March 2014, two decades after the collapse of the Soviet Union, Vladimir Putin attacked Ukraine and seized and declared Crimea as part of Russian territory under the pretext of protecting ethnic Russians.

Relatedness is to blame for the rival territorial claims for the resource-rich waters of the South China Sea by Japan, Indonesia, Singapore, Vietnam, the Philippines, Brunei, Taiwan and Malaysia lately. Relatedness is also culpable for the long-simmering tensions and vicious fighting between the Sunni, Shiite (and sometimes Kurdish) Muslim sects. Relatedness is also liable for the long-drawn Israeli-Palestinian conflict.

Conflicts and wars fundamentally change the global order. The First World War destroyed lives; four empires (Germany, Austria-Hungary, Russia and Ottoman rule); introduced chemical weapons; and brought millions of women into the work force. The Second World War cost more than 10 million lives; obliterated cities; bankrupted Britain and France; destroyed Germany; and introduced nuclear weapons with the bombing of Japan's Hiroshima and Nagasaki.

Realists such as Morgenthau (1948) characterize the international ecosystem as anarchic observing that no sovereign authority exists above the state. Each state must therefore look out for its own interests above all. The implication is that states battle for power and latitude.

But, according to connectedness, the international system is orderly, benign and well-intentioned. The will of the universe governs the regular interaction of states and non-state actors.

States (knowingly or unknowingly) do not thirst for power or self-interest. States struggle to fulfill the edict of the universe. Therefore, the current pre-occupation with boundaries, economic exclusion, espionage, artillery and guns, unmanned stealth drones and possession of nuclear technology are thoughtless. The role of the state and politics is to sustain life.

The state is a spatial entity that facilitates the sustenance of life within a defined geographical jurisdiction. However, the prevalence of political mobilizations that appeal to narrow political bases (relatedness) implies that most politicians lack the incentive to pursue higher ideals unless they are prompted to do so. This is urgent especially with the emergence chemical, biological and nuclear arsenals. Progressive non-state organizations are in the enviable position of doing the prompting.

Civil society, media and academia have unique policy decision roles to overcome politics shaped by fear, insecurity and hatreds, ensure fidelity to the rule of law and guarantee accountability to the will of the universe, which is to preserve life.

Organized non-state entities emerged to promote consultation, participation and collective interest. Notable organized entities include professional associations, interest groups, NGOs, corporations, companies and states. The UN was formed to mediate the jostling among individuals, groups and states. The UN was meant to bring about order in the state system.

The effectiveness of the UN is however mixed. The cold war was the first real test for the UN. The Cold War led to the collapse of the former Soviet Union. The New International Order (NIO) that replaced the bipolar system of the Cold War premised on international law and international norms (characterized by the peaceful settlement of disputes through international courts, universal human rights, international criminal justice, and free trade and investment) seems not to have run out of steam.

Today it is apparent that the UN is completely at loss whenever a conflict involves the permanent members of the

UN Security Council or when it has to do with self-determination.

Global political connectedness can act as a check on aggression by ushering in perfect democracy. Political uncertainties arising from the absence of shared goals and value system contribute to fragmentation along boundaries.

Civil society, media and academia may have to shift global relations away from zero-sum issues (geopolitics and war) toward win-win ones (free trade and investment, neighborhood tourism and conferencing, neighborhood diplomacy and collective life preservation).

Global diplomacy must no longer be concerned with boundaries, military bases, diversity, national self-determination, or spheres of influence.

Devolution is a universal trend. Archimedes (287 BCE – 212 BCE) pledged to move the world if he would be given a point of support (a fulcrum and a compact spot on which to stand).

To paraphrase Archimedes, every point can be regarded as the center of the universe. In a different way, from the neighborhood (spatial location) as the fulcrum one can stir the universe.

Power is a remarkable form of connectedness. Accommodating power (synergy) is the conduit of life. To prevent war in the state system the grassroots must shape the choice of leaders and leadership. People who are rewarded with public office for successfully or otherwise for violently persecuting hegemony and or grievances along fault lines almost always never change tact. Without faultlines, issues take precedence. Without divisive human groups, humanity gets the opportunity to reward good governance and punish mediocre leadership on a world scale.

Fukuyama wrongly suggested that liberal democracy is the only way to democratically organize society politically. Liberal democracy is actually merely transitional democracy. The hitch is that liberal democracies supposedly respect the supremacy of the will of the people (Rousseau, 2012), which oftentimes is not the will of the universe.

The failure of liberal democracy project is apparent in countries as varied as Sri Lanka, Pakistan, Bangladesh, Nepal, India, just to mention a few.

Indeed, Peter Geschiere in *The Perils of Belonging* explores the connection between globalization and the emergence of local exclusionary identities.

Relatedness is responsible for our ancient survival instincts (ego-centrism) as well as our need to belong to exclusive groups for survival, power and resources. Connectedness is about inclusiveness and collective survival.

Fukuyama predicated that the post-historical society would look frighteningly nihilistic. Following Friedrich Nietzsche, Fukuyama's description of the "last man" resembles a narcissistic consumer with no greater aspirations beyond the next trip to the shopping precinct.

Fukuyama's reality (the dictates of a fruitless ideology) can only materialize in the absence of widely shared set of values. Many people in many parts of the world are already beginning to turn away from consumerism and toward other sources of satisfaction. Concern for the welfare of others (charity work) that is now widespread represents connectedness.

LINGUISTIC CONNECTEDNESS

Communication is critical for collaboration, cooperation, and knowledge sharing. Language is a mental faculty that shapes and facilitates the sharing of experience and the expression of knowledge.

Humans invented spoken, written and artificial languages to organize, store, share and communicate their thoughts and experiences of the surrounding world and to facilitate the manipulation of nature to sustain life. Languages are bridges of life.

The most-spoken languages in the world include Chinese (Mandarin), English, Spanish, Hindustani/Hindi, Arabic, Russian, Portuguese, Japanese, German and French.

The world is witnessing prolonged and regular contact between speakers of one or more languages in the process that may lead to linguistic homogeneity to facilitate world trade, diplomacy and increased human contact worldwide.

The drive for a perfect language represents the progress towards lingual (universal) connectedness. All human beings will ultimately speak the same language giving us more control over the world around us.

ECONOMIC CONNECTEDNESS

The desire for connectedness is the fundamental driver of economic systems, trade and markets. Points of trade have facilitated human interaction, sharing and exchange since the dawn of humankind. However, given the world's imperial history, each divide wants to become the world's dominant economic power. The resulting zero-sum game constrains world resources leading to undesirable outcomes.

Today, out of the seven billion people living on Earth, more than a billion people subsist in extreme poverty and about three billion people are categorized as poor. Regrettably, suggested policy alternatives do not effectively deal with the core problem of world economy, which is the lack of a shared goal or value system.

Scientists have concentrated on the choice between markets (neo-liberal economics), public action (Keynesianism, unemployment benefits and Socialism) and the mixed model (statist model/market socialism as in China) and forgotten the role of the nonprofit sector. On this score, connectedness fairs much better than globalization (relatedness).

The market economy is the most enterprising mechanism established by humankind to facilitate interdependence.

Geographical boundaries between markets are being erased. The market economy rewards actors with profits, wages and recognition for providing goods and services to others. However, scarcity, a core principle of unchecked capitalism, is an interesting concept.

Scarcity of capital[13] in the wake of relatedness fuels competition in the human society clouding the importance of the market economy serving the common good. Consequently, the marketplace characterized by speculative capital flows has inevitably not succeeded in bringing about greater justice and inclusiveness in the world.

The state as a spatial entity legislates, executes, dispenses justice and deploys the necessary infrastructure. However, in the absence of a global monetary system (universal currency), the state is almost always faced with the choice between jobs (inflation) and economic growth. This explains why trickle-down economics scores poorly in the war on poverty, inequality and historical neglect.

John Rawls in *A Theory of Justice* (1971) used though experiments to justify collective fairness dubbed "justice as fairness". He observes that if we were to picture ourselves in

---

[13] Capital is existing monetized wealth

the original position behind a veil of ignorance (in the worst case scenario) not knowing how we will turn out to be in terms of societal position, material affluence, gender, religious persuasion, social status, disability status etc. we would want to construct a society that is fair and just. If there must be some form of undue advantage it should accrue to the least advantaged members of society.

As a substitute to focusing on the non-discriminatory sharing of wealth Rawls believed in justice as opportunity. He demonstrated that we are all endowed with natural assets. Success in life depends upon whether we have been afforded the opportunity to make use of our aptitudes and talents.

Rawls puts a premium on the value of just institutions, mutual aid and collective interests. His thought process has patently influenced real world politics namely the welfare state; affirmative action; Obama's senatorial and presidential victories; and ObamaCare.

Connectedness puts humanity at the center of economic activity. According to connectedness, the universe's greatest asset is its people. People are wealth.

Walking around hamlets, villages and remote rural neighborhoods, one easily notices signs of endemic poverty, joblessness and historical neglect. Increasingly, most people want to live and work in cities and urban neighborhoods. People move to urban areas in search of jobs, economic empowerment and a better life. Subsequently, wealth has been concentrated in privileged urban areas.

Economic growth is not enough to alleviate poverty and inequality. Creation of sufficient income opportunities is no doubt one of the most effective ways of poverty alleviation and redressing extreme inequality. Perfect employment can be achieved worldwide by the nonprofit sector creating new markets though innovative infrastructural platforms that facilitates governments and the private sector to offer goods and services in remote and rural environments worldwide.

Instead of having unidirectional rural-urban migration, villages and remote environments can be turned into cities to spark and increase the world's urbanization threefold.

Connectedness centers the collaboration of the public, private and non-profit sectors to cultivate a shared goal and value system in efforts to manage world economic disparity, end persistent conflict, prop up infrastructure in rural, remote and marginalized areas and alleviate waste and other sub-optimal outcomes around the world.

The crucial ingredient for sustainable worldwide economic growth is massive investment in people, infrastructure (urbanizing rural environments by turning hamlets into cities) and cultivation of better social relations. The point is to ensure that every human is of benefit to each and every other human being and the world around us.

One of the costs the world pays for erecting and maintaining identities is economic fluctuations.

Economic fluctuations are a permanent fixture of the world economy just like the way identity struggles fluctuate so do currencies. The multiple currency system is meant to satisfy our ego. However, the bitter truth is that today the world transacts in dollars. All these other national payment and settlement platforms only facilitate speculation (deflation and inflation) and of course unemployment.

HISTORICAL CONNECTEDNESS

History is more than an academic discipline and/or a methodical process of inquiry to interpret and explain the past. History is deliberate and consequential. History is the record of past events as humankind, other life forms, and non-life forms struggle to sustain life *ad infinitum.*

Most of the available scientific evidence suggests that human life began 4.7 billion years ago. Until around 11,000 BCE, at the end of the last Ice Age, humans were still living as Stone Age hunter/gatherers. Steadily humans developed agriculture, herding, metallurgy, language, art, religion, complex political organization, spacecraft, nuclear weapons and the Internet. Soon, practically everything will connect to the internet raising the possibility of home automation, integrated transportation, and programmed healthcare.

All these discoveries and developments cannot be considered chance events. We study the high points and injustices of history to determine the discernable pattern in historical events.

Through time the course of history has been diverted in every possible way. The reason is simple. Most people in parts of the world explicitly subscribe to relatedness. Even historians do have agendas and do select sources with the intent of proving certain preconceived notions. History is therefore never truly objective.

Relatedness greatly influences our understanding of the complex human past. Because of relatedness, history has regularly been employed to create division rather than cohesion. This means that in the making of history, at certain points there is scope for the misrepresentation, distortion and manipulation of historical events to serve political causes.

But perhaps the main reason why people resort to relatedness is because of their incapacity to explain the broad pattern of human history.

History in a wider sense is the entirety of all past events. Realistically, history is the known past. History is purpose-driven. History chronicles the development of the human awareness of their connectedness with the rest of the universe.

MEANING IN PERIODIZATION[14] OF UNIVERSAL HISTORY

TIMELINES	FEATURES	RELATEDNESS
PREHISTORIC[15] (2,500,000-10,000 BCE) **Stone [16]Age** (The hunting and foraging era characterized by the fashioning and use of stone for tool-making)	**Paleolithic (2,500,000-200,000 BCE)** **(Old Stone Age)** ❖ This period witnessed the evolution of Australopithecus, an extinct genus of hominids. ❖ During this period, humans were hunters and gatherers subsisting on hunting wild animals and birds, fishing, and collecting wild fruits, vegetables, tubers, nuts, and berries. ❖ The earliest stone tools included the Oldowan and later the Acheulian.	
	Mesolithic (200,000-40,000 BCE) **(Middle Stone Age)** ❖ Characterized by more advanced hunter-gathering, fishing and rudimentary forms of cultivation.	
	Neolithic (40,000-10,000 BCE) **(New stone age)** ❖ Begins with the introduction of farming (cereal cultivation), animal domestication and permanent settlements (sedentary living)	
HISTORIC **ANCIENT** **(Bronze & Iron Age)** 10000 BCE-500 CE (Emergence of civilization) The fall of Rome marks the end of ancient history.	**Bronze Age (3300- 300 BCE)** ❖ Characterized by the development of metallurgy (i.e. copper and tin mining and smelting), cremation burials, settled communities and the emergence of important ancient river valley civilizations: Sumerian - Euphrates and the Tigris; Ancient Egypt – the Nile; the Indus Valley- the Indus; Ancient Greek - Aegean Sea; Chinese - Yellow River and He Huang River; the Aztecs in central America and the Incas in the Andes.	
	Iron Age (300 BCE – 500 CE) ❖ Marked by the processing of iron ore to produce iron or steel tools and weapons. ❖ Also the rise of Phoenicia, Ancient Greek & Ancient Rome (Mediterranean/Europe); Seleucid/Parthian (Middle East); Meroe, Aksum, Kingdom of Kush, Kingdom of Benin, and Great Zimbabwe (Africa); Vedic period (India); Zhou Dynasty (China); and formative, Preclassic & Classic (Americas).	

---

[14] Periodization is the partition of the human past into distinct time eras, periods, epochs and or ages. The two major phases of world history are relatedness and connectedness.

[15] Prehistory is the period of human existence prior to the development and use of writing systems. However, the increased reliance on archaeology, anthropology, linguistics, oral traditions, genetics and geology besides written sources has helped blur the distinction between prehistory and history.

[16] Christian Jürgensen Thomsen (1788–1865) is credited for having originated the three-age system (Stone Age, Bronze Age, and Iron Age) for classifying and studying prehistoric and ancient societies.

MEDIEVAL Lasted from 476 to 1500 CE Dark Ages (500 – 1000 CE)	❖ The beginning of middle ages in Mediterranean/Europe starts with the fall of the Roman Empire in 476 CE which meant much of Europe was characterized by confusion as local kings and rulers tried to seize power. This was actually the start of the Dark Ages. ❖ Elsewhere, in 570 CE Prophet Muhammad was born contributing to the Islamic Golden Age under Sasaria caliphates. Prophet Muhammad died in 632 CE. ❖ The period also witnessed Axumite Empire (Africa), Imperial China, Middle kingdoms (India) and Maya, Inca and Aztecs empires (Classic, post-classic & Pre-Columbian Americas).	
MODERN[17] 1500 – 1960 CE)	**Renaissance (1500 -1517 CE)** ❖ Johannes Gutenberg's invention of the printing press in 1444 signaled the start of the Renaissance since many more people now had access to books, especially the Bible. ❖ Rebirth of knowledge (Secular rebellion) ❖ Leonardo da Vinci's painting of the *Last Super* (1498) *and Mona Lisa* (1505). ❖ Modern state system introduced with the publication of Machiavelli's *The Prince* (1513) **Reformation (1517-1600 CE)** ❖ Spiritual rebellion led by reformers like Martin Luther, John Calvin and who challenged papal authority, indulgences and questioned the Catholic Church's ability to define Christian practice. **Enlightenment (1600 – 1960)** ❖ Scientific Revolution (Bacon, Copernicus, Kepler, Galileo, Newton), Age of discovery and Exploration and later the rise of intellectuals (Darwin, Mendel, Descartes, Leibniz, Kant, Einstein, Oppeihmer, Kuhn, Feyerabend, Ricardo, Smith, Marx, etc.). ❖ Political Revolution (Hobbes, Mill, Rousseau, Locke, Paine – English, American and French Revolutions). ❖ Industrial Revolution contributing to Imperialism (Slavery, Classical imperialism, Colonialism, Neo-colonialism & later globalization) ❖ Major wars (WWI, WWII and later Cold War) ❖ End of European colonialism (nationalism and decolonization)	
POSTMODERN (1960-2000 CE)	Transition to Connectedness Major thinkers include Heidegger, Derrida, Foucault, Lyotard, Rorty & Kellner	
CONNECTEDNESS **(2015 CE - ?)**		

---

[17] Post-medieval Europe

Pre-history

Understanding the past appears to be a universal human need, and the telling of history has emerged independently in almost all parts of the world.

Narrative[18] was traditionally the main rhetorical device used by historians. During prehistory, before writing became the norm, historical knowledge was orally transmitted from generation to generation through fairy tales, legends, riddles, proverbs, rituals, drama, song, dance, chants, jokes, art, and in the genealogies of ancestors for the purpose of informing future generations about past human activities (Ki-Zerbo, 1990; Mazrui, 1999; Ogot, 1999).

Oral tradition[19] is one of the only ways through which the contemporary world gets to know what happened in these non-writing societies. Other tools or sources that have been used by historians to gather, preserve and explore the history of pre-literate geographical locations include archaeological research, genetic studies, anthropology and linguistics.

The invention of writing greatly advanced the quest to systematically record human activities. The earliest writing

---

[18] Narrative refers to the transmission of historical tradition without written instruction.
[19] Oral tradition was either prose or verse narratives.

systems include the Sumerian cuneiform (from 3100 BCE), Egyptian hieroglyphics from 3000 BCE, Indus script (2500 BCE), Chinese writing (1600 BCE), the Phonetic alphabet (1500 BCE), the Arabic script (500 BCE) and Mesoamerican scripts (200 CE). Other early writing schemes include the Meroetic scripts, Amharic in Ethiopia, Vai writing in Liberia and Sierra Leone, and the Nsibidi script of the Cross River basin of Nigeria, among many others.

The invention of writing birthed recorded history. The emphasis of written history was on the critical examination of primary sources and other evidence. That being the case, written history is largely based on earlier unwritten scholarship such as oral tradition.

Hellenic (Greek) Historiography[20]

In the Hellenic world (Ancient Greece), around the 4th millennium BCE, the search for cause and effect took precedence over mere accumulation of records. Ancient thinkers reasoned that events don't just happen. Even accidents don't just occur. Events are caused. There's always a

---

[20] Historiography refers to the changing interpretations of historical events in the works of individual historians. It is the history of historical writing.

series of events leading up to the occurrence of events. History is the search for veiled cause(s) for past events.

Herodotus[21] of Halicarnassus (484-425 BCE) authored *The Histories* (440 BCE) to document Greco-Persian Wars. He personally sourced for evidence by travelling extensively. Herodotus concluded that divinity largely directs historical events.

Shortly afterward, Thucydides (460-395 BCE) in his classic study of *The Peloponnesian War* between Athens and Sparta and their surrogates emphasized firsthand inquiry but largely eliminated divine causality in his writings. Thucydides blamed hubris for the 27 years bloody spectacle that was fought from 431 to 404 BCE (Hanson, 2006).

Thucydides emphasized the critical role human actors, their choices and actions play in shaping the direction of history. He greatly influenced subsequent historical writings for distinguishing between cause and immediate origins of an event.

---

[21] Cicero considered Herodotus as the 'the father of history'.

Greco-Roman Historiography

Philip II of Macedon, the father of Alexander the Great, defeated an alliance of Thebans and Athenians in 338 BCE, ushering in Greco-Roman historiography.

Two years later, his son, Alexander the Great, took the reins of the Greek Kingdom of Macedonia. For the next 13 years, Alexander the Great was involved in an empire-building campaign that drastically altered the history of the world, birthing the Hellenistic period.

The Hellenistic Period[22] began in 323 BCE with Alexander's death and ended in 31 BCE when Octavian (later Augustus[23]) defeated Anthony and Cleopatra the rulers of Ptolemaic Egypt[24] at the battle of Actium. Earlier on, the Seleucid dynasty (Syria), Attalid dynasty of Pergamum (Asia Minor) and Antigonid dynasty (Greek peninsula) had caved in with the rise of the Roman Empire.

Hellenization was outstanding in thought during this period. The major schools of thought were the Stoicism, Skepticism and Epicureanism.

---

[22] Greek colonization of Europe, Asia and Africa

[23] Augustus (63 BCE – 14 CE) became the first emperor of Rome in 27 BCE. He led Rome's transformation from republic to empire during the tumultuous years following the assassination of his great-uncle and adoptive father Julius Caesar.

[24] Egypt was the last of the territories that Alexander the Great had once ruled.

Greco-Roman historiography traces its maturation to Polybius (203–120 BCE). Polybius wrote on the history of the rise of Rome to world prominence. He managed to successfully harmonize the Greek and Roman points of view.

Other notable historians and essayists who subscribed to the Greco-Roman tradition include Ptolemy I, Livy, Virgil, Plutarch, Tacitus and Flavius Josephus.

Ptolemy 1 (367–283 BCE) was a historian, one of the heir kings to the empire of Alexander the Great, and founded the Ptolemaic dynasty in Egypt. He moved Egypt's capital from Memphis to Alexandria. Ptolemy made Alexandria the intellectual center of the Mediterranean and attracted notable scholars such as Euclid and Archimedes. Almost three hundred years after the death Ptolemy 1, Egypt was conquered by the Romans (Julius Caesar) in 31 BCE.

Virgil (70-19 BCE) wrote the *Aeneid*, an epic which narrates the founding of Rome and declares the Roman mission to develop the world under divine guidance.

Livy (59 BCE– 17 CE) in *History of Rome from its Foundation* recorded the rise of Rome from city-state to empire.

Plutarch (46–127 CE) in *Parallel Lives* wrote biographies of legendary Greeks and Romans emphasizing their human strengths and weaknesses.

Tacitus (56–117 CE) in the *Annals* and the *Histories* recounted the reigns of the Roman Emperors Tiberius, Claudius and Nero, among others. His narration recorded the -Jewish revolt (66–70 CE) and mentioned Jesus.

Flavius Josephus (37-100 CE) recorded the Jewish-Roman relations. The writings of Josephus are considered authoritative because he was an eyewitness and or participant in the historical events he documented. In *The Jewish War* (75 CE), Josephus narrates the Jewish mutinies against Roman rulership (66–70 CE). In *Antiquities of the Jews* (94 CE), he narrates the history of the Jews.

The historical writings of Tacitus and Josephus represent the earliest sources on the historical Jesus and the soon after emergence of Early Christianity.

Jesus of Nazareth actively preached and was arrested in Jerusalem, a territory in Roman Judea. Jesus was first brought before Pontius Pilate, the prefect of Roman Judea from 26 CE to 36 CE, for sentencing. Pilate in the beginning handed him over to Herod Antipas[25] (21 BCE – 39 CE).

Herod Antipa ruled over Galilee (and Perea) for 42 years from 4 BCE to 39 CE. Most of Jesus' life and ministry (and later crucifixion and death) happened in Galilee. Galilee was a Roman client state under Emperor Tiberius.

Historical and gospel accounts state that Antipas refused to preside over the trial of Jesus and sent him back to Pilate's court.

Pilate initially refused to convict Jesus of treason, but was left with no choice but to condemn him to death by an out of control crowd. Jesus was eventually crucified and buried.

The trial and crucifixion of Jesus gave birth to Christianity. Christianity introduced turn-the-other-cheek doctrine to replace the eye-to-an eye and tooth-for-a-tooth dogmas.

Medieval Christendom Historiography

---

[25] Herod Antipas was the son of King Herod the Great. His father, Herod the Great was a Roman client king of Judea before it was divided into Judea, Samaria and Idumea; Galilee and Peraea; and territories East of Jordan.

Christianity emerged in the mid first century CE (about 2000 years ago) in Judea (now Palestine and Israel) (Johnson, 1979). Judea was under the rulership of the emperor of Rome. Roman rule and Rome's polytheistic beliefs were loathed. Predictably, Jesus' birth was seen as the fulfillment of the prophecy on the promised Messiah (savior).

The Christian religion is premised on the life, teachings, death, and resurrection of Jesus Christ. Christians are Jesus' followers. Unlike the three predominant Jewish sects (the Pharisees, the Sadducees and the Essenes), the Christian faith was open to Jews and non-Jews alike.

From the start, Christianity stood out because of Jesus' message of hope (and love) and its inclusivity. No wonder, despite relentless random and officially sanctioned persecutions by the leadership of the Roman Empire, Christianity continued to grow in leaps and bounds. Predictably, in 312 CE, the Roman Emperor Constantine 1 became a Christian. And, Christianity became the authorized religion of the Roman Empire 70 years later, during the reign of emperor Theodosius. From thereon, the state and religion (the Roman Catholic Church) became one and the same thing, and Christians were no longer persecuted.

The expansion of the Christian faith and its superior status in the Roman Empire led to the re-emergence of the intervention of divinity in human affairs. Medieval Christendom historiography introduced the idea of a linear (universal) history that progresses according to a (universal) divine plan (Bede[26], 1990). God's plan to salvage humankind unfolds through universal and inclusive human history; encompasses everyone anywhere.

Medieval Christendom historiography had a universal perspective preparing it for its future civilizing (imperial) mission when Europe expanded to dominate the Americas, Asia and Africa.

During the medieval period, popes claiming secular and spiritual authority imposed their will on daily life. However, sleaze, self-indulgence and egotism in the church hierarchy became routine. The popes, from 1095 to 1290, endorsed a series of bloody encounters (the crusades) to repel Muslim advances.

Many years later, Catholicism got entangled in a series of wars with the protestant movement during the Protestant Reformation led by protestant reformers such as Johannes

---

[26] Bede (672/673 – 735 CE) penned the *Ecclesiastical History of the English People* (731 CE) highlighting this distinct medieval Christendom historiography.

Hus, Martin Luther, John Calvin and Huldrych Zwingli. The reformers were insistent that the Bible has supremacy over church tradition. The Reformation effectively dismantled the power of the Roman Catholic Church and helped open the door to the post-medieval Europe.

The Christian faith managed to expand to cover almost the entire globe, and to become the world's largest religion partially assisted by European intervention in Africa, Asia and the Americas.

Today the three major divisions of Christianity are Roman Catholicism, Eastern Orthodoxy and Protestantism.

Medieval Islamic Historiography

Islam began in Mecca (Arabia) in the 7th century CE (about 1400 years ago) through Prophet Muhammad (570 - 632 CE). Muslims are those who subscribe to the Islamic faith.

The Islamic Golden Age began and ended with the reign of the Abbasid caliph Harun ar-Rashid (786 to 809 CE) with the inauguration and collapse of the House of Wisdom in Baghdad. The Abbasid Caliphate collapsed with the Mongol invasions and the Sack of Baghdad in 1258. This period witnessed monumental strides in science, technology, medicine, philosophy and art (Lombard, 2003; Al-Djazairi, 2006).

Islamic writing emerged with the reconstruction of the Prophet Muhammad's life following his death. One of the most important historian and historiographer on Islamic caliphates was Ibn Khaldun[27] (1332–1406). Ibn Khaldun was critical of redundant superstition and uncritical acceptance of (military) historical data.

Ibn Khaldun in the *Muqaddimah* (Introduction) (1406 CE) originated the idea that civilizations rise and fall. His cyclical theory on the growth and decline of civilizations later found use in the study of the expansion and collapse of the Ottoman Empire and the decline of Byzantium. Khaldun also greatly influenced Edward Gibbon's *The History of the Decline and Fall of the Roman Empire (1776)*, Oswald Spengler's *The Decline of the West* (1918) and William L. Shirer's *The Rise and Fall of the Third Reich: A History of Nazi Germany* (1960).

Ibn Khaldun noted the historical role of successor Islamic caliphates (the state). According to Khaldun, caliphates decline when successive shifts in power regress into absolute

---

[27] Khaldun is often celebrated as the father of the philosophy of history.

monarchy; when more than one caliph is nominated; and or when the nominated caliph is not a direct descendant of Prophet Muhammad's family line.

Generally, Islam has been a source of unity and synergy throughout the world. In fact, Islam is the second largest religion in the world. The reason as to why this is the case can be found in the five pillars of Islam: the declaration of faith; praying five times a day; giving money to charity; fasting; and a pilgrimage to Mecca (at least once in a person's lifetime).

However, Islam has also been the source of disunity and schism. The explanation for this is that most Muslims are Sunni (85%), Shia (15%) or Khawarij.

Sunnis embrace the first four elected Muslim caliphs (Abu Bakr, Uthman ibn al-Affan and Umar ibn al-Khattab) as the rightful successors to Muhammad. Accordingly, Sunnis believe that anyone who is righteous and just could be a caliph so long as s/he is voted by Muslims and or their representatives and act according to the Qur'an and the Hadith. Predictably, Sunni Islam is the largest Muslim denomination composed of 85% of all Muslims.

Shia's subscribe to the view that Muhammad appointed his son-in-law, Ali ibn Abi Talib, as his successor and only certain descendants of Ali could be Imams. Accordingly, Ali ibn Abi Talib was the first Imam (leader). They reject the legitimacy of the previous Muslim caliphs on the understanding that a Caliph should not be elected by the community rather must be Prophet Muhammad's direct descendant. Unsurprisingly, the Shia constitutes a paltry 15% of all Muslims.

Khawarij is an immoderate sect that initially supported Muhammad's son-in-law and cousin Ali ibn Abi Talib but afterward rejected him.

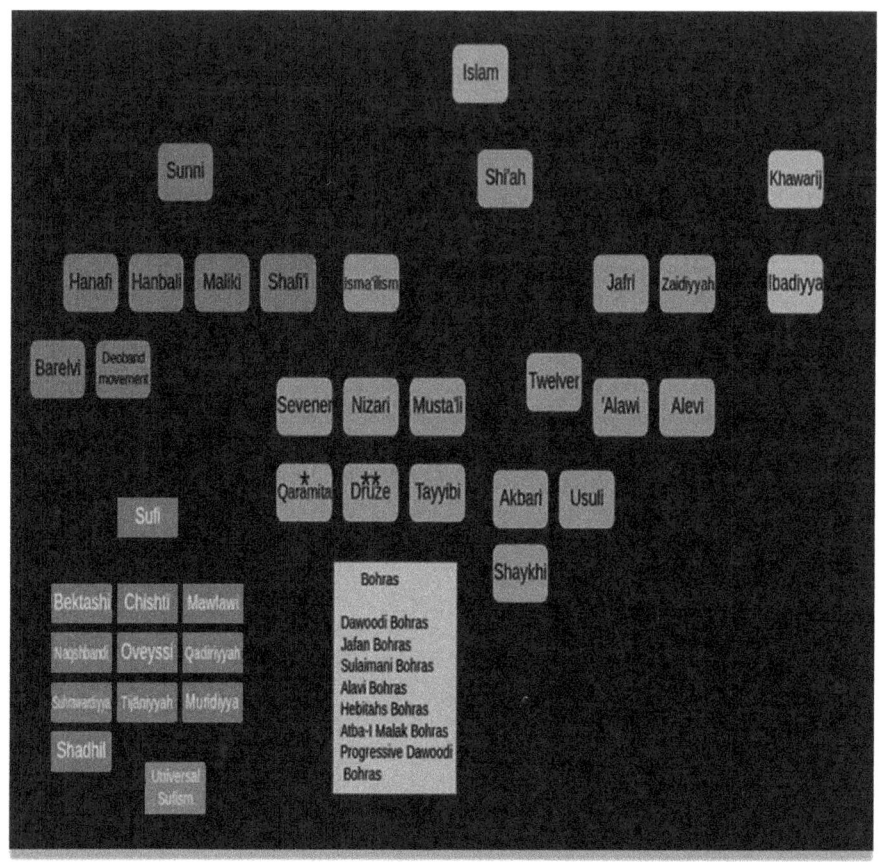

Fig 7: Major Islamic Sects and Branches

Source: Wikipedia

Post-Medieval European Historiography

During Renaissance, the period that immediately followed the Middle Ages, God was replaced with human actors as the center of historical events. This was a period of rebirth of learning after the medieval centuries that were considered superstitious.

Humanism and the gradual secularization of critical thought influenced post-medieval European historiography. History from this period onward was written about states (or nations).

Niccolò Machiavelli[28] (1469–1527 CE) pioneered theorization on state power and politics. In *The Prince* (1513) he dealt with monarchal rule and how devious politicians resort to any means (particularly deceit and fear) as they scheme to institute and maintain total authority. Machiavelli to a great extent influenced later thinkers such as Thomas Hobbes, Francis Bacon, Baruch Spinoza, Jean-Jacques Rousseau, John Locke and Antonio Gramsci.

From the fifteenth century, European explorers, traders, sailors, missionaries, and other travelers ushered in the historiography of imperialism.

Hegel (1770–1831 CE), after medieval Christendom, re-introduced the linear study of world historical development. Previous historians (such as Ibn Khaldun) had focused on cyclical historical development and majorly dealt with the rise and decline of caliphates (rulers, nations and empires). Hegel

---

[28] Machiavelli is often considered the father of modern political theory.

noted that thought (ideas) push historical progress forward. For Hegel, history is the development of the ideas of freedom, reason, self-awareness and recognition (Hegel, 1976; 2004; 2014).

Hegel concluded that the human struggle for liberty, self-understanding and respect reach its climax during the French Revolution (thought and action). The French people gave birth to current-day constitutionalism with their chants 'Liberte, Egalite and Fraternite' (Freedom, Equality and Brotherhood).

Karl Marx[29] (1818–1883) in *A Contribution to the Critique of Political Economy* (1859) suggested that the economy is the most important part of society. Therefore, history is determined by the rise, development and decline of different modes of production. Unlike Hegel, Marx observed that human activity, rather than thought, moves world history.

Marx, however, in *The Communist Manifesto* (1848) noted that the progression of human history is often hindered by class consciousness. For him, the history of the world involves the struggle among social classes (rather than conflicts between powerful individuals or states). This is on the understanding

---

[29] Karl Marx was not just interested in studying the world; he hoped to change it, "philosophers have only interpreted the world in various ways; the point is, to change it".

that capitalism is both an economic and political system. The capitalist economic system creates a wealthy class of owners and a poor class of workers. Certain social institutions such as churches, prisons and schools help maintain the division between the powerful and the powerless.

In *Das Kapital* (1867), Marx thought that connectedness (a world without classes) could be achieved through a socialist revolution and the consequent triumph of communism. Marxist thought has greatly influenced labour unions, co-operatives, political parties and intellectual movements worldwide.

Vladimir Lenin (1870-1924) was excited with Marxism. However, he deviated with the Marxist model of history which suggested that every society has to experience primitive communalism, slavery, feudalism and capitalism before socialism could be established. Besides, whereas Karl Marx had predicted that the industrial working will foment a revolution, Lenin thought that peasantry in Russia could do just that. To achieve this end, it was necessary to form a small vanguard party composed of professionals to overthrow the Tsar regime in Russia.

Lenin in *Imperialism: The Highest Stage of Capitalism* (1917), suggests that great power rivalry was responsible for colonialism and WW1. For him, the global development of the capitalist economy is by design characterized by conflicts and antagonism. To facilitate connectedness, he strongly advocated for the right of all people to determine the shape and conditions of their national, political and social existence.

Lenin's stance on self-determination of all peoples was to play out in the post-World War II matrix. The East-West polarization immediately after World War II, as a result of the Cold War, made it a necessity for the capitalist and the socialist blocs to look for allies in low income countries.

Neo-Marxists continued from where Lenin left in their criticism of global capitalism. Neo-Marxism frameworks amended and extended classical Marxism to explain why in the current world there are countless high income countries in Europe and America and hardly any high income country in some parts of Asia, Africa and Latin America. The solution suggested was the disengagement with the capitalist West.

The capitalist West had a different explanation for the prevalence of low income countries in Asia, Africa and Latin America. According to modernization theory, all societies progress through similar stages of development. W. W. Rostow (1916–2003) was the most influential modernization theorist. In *The Stages of Economic Growth: A Non-Communist Manifesto* (1960) he suggested that all societies pass through five stages: traditional society, economic growth, take-off, drive to maturity and age of high mass consumption. Today's low-income areas are in a similar situation to that of today's high-income areas at some time in the past.

The Modernization school opined that underdevelopment arose from domestic causes namely customs, overpopulation, modest investment and or the general lack of incentive to move society forward. To accelerate development it was necessary to scale up investment, technology transfers, and encourage closer integration into the world market.

Modernization School of development was tasked to promote economic growth and political stability in low income countries. The approach taken by modernization theorists ushered in a period characterized by industrialization through import subsidies that contributed to a short period of economic expansion in the 1950s in Latin America. However, subsequent decades were characterized by widespread poverty and economic stagnation (unemployment, inflation, declining terms of trade, etc).

Partly as a result of sub-optimal results of policies based on the modernization theories and the crisis of orthodox Marxism, neo-Marxist perspectives under the banner of dependency, underdevelopment and unequal exchange emerged to critic and offer alternatives to modernization. The major neo-Marxist proponents were Raul Prebisch, Paul Baran, Andre Gunder Frank, Walter Rodney, Samir Amin, F.H. Cardoso and the non-Marxist Immanuel Wallerstein.

Dependency theory approached underdevelopment as a historical process (history of imperialism in the form of slavery, colonialism and neo-colonialism) and not as a circumstance that is native to low income countries. So, underdevelopment arose from external and not internal causes. The perspective also rejected the view that low-income countries are simply primeval versions of high-income countries observing that their current state of affairs arises from the fact that they are underdogs in the international capitalist economy.

Andre Gunder Frank's central contention was that underdevelopment arises because of the division between metropoles and satellites. Poor countries are impoverished and rich ones enriched by the way poor countries are integrated into the world system. Through unequal trade, resources flow from peripheral poor and underdeveloped countries (Africa, much of Asia and Latin America) to a core of wealthy countries (North America, Europe and Australia), enriching the last at the expense of the earlier.

Walter Rodney was another important proponent of the dependency model. Rodney in *How Europe Underdeveloped Africa* (1972) persuasively points out that Africa became integrated in the world capitalist system from the sixteenth century. From this point on, Africa has been a victim of exploitation starting with slavery, colonialism and then neo-colonialism. Africa's underdevelopment results from the uneven development in earlier centuries. European slave trade, the expansion of Europe overseas and subsequent exploitative practices interfered with Africa's historical development causing considerable dislocation and disruption in Africa's vibrant economic, social and political structures (Rodney, 2011).

Paul A. Baran (1909–1964) in *The Political Economy of Growth* (1957) using the concept surplus value significantly contributed to underdevelopment theory. At the core of this framework is the satellite (agriculture) vis-a-viz metropole (industry) dichotomy. Baran observed that their existed dual economies. Satellite countries were largely predominated by extremely low productive agricultural sectors while metropole countries had industrial sectors that were highly productive. Metropole countries preferred the status quo because satellite economies were sources of raw materials and markets for finished products. State intervention was necessary to escape dependency.

Samir Amin (1931-?) publicized the notion of centre and periphery. The centre needed a peripheral economy to produce goods for comfort, generate surplus and foreign currency instead of producing for own consumption or to stimulate neighborhood development (Samir, 1974; 1976; 1977). Deprived countries supply natural resources and inexpensive labour; serve as a destination for obsolete technology and markets for industrial countries, without which the latter could not maintain the lifestyle they enjoy.

Fernando Cardoso opined that the world market and other external factors differently impact countries with divergent internal conditions. Therefore, it is fallacious to treat all dependent economies as being homogenous. Internal conditions and factors largely determine whether a peripheral country can experience dependent associated development (1977). Using this perspective, it became possible to explain the phenomenal rise of the Asian tigers (Malaysia, Singapore, Taiwan and South Korea).

Immanuel Wallerstein's non-Marxist approach categorized countries into three main clusters: center, semi-peripheral and peripheral (Wallerstein, 1974; 2004). A country's development outlook is determined by its position in the international economic and political system. The fact that growth prospects depend on the nature of global system rather than internal structures means that no country is associated with a permanent cluster. This approach in a different way also managed to capture semi-peripheral economic status of Asian tigers.

Neo-Marxist and the non-Marxist Wallerstein take the position that high income countries actively perpetuate a state of dependence. To escape dependency, low income countries have to partially or completely de-link from the international capitalist system.

Postmodernist and Postcolonial Historiography

The era of decolonization and the immediate post-independence years witnessed the era of nationalist, liberalist and neo-Marxist historiography.

In the late 1050s and early 1960s, national historiography emphasized the study of the liberation movements, the national liberation revolutions, and the struggle against modern-day imperialism. The nationalist elite were united by the quest for freedom. But the nationalist consensus soon broke down immediately self-rule was attained. While relatedness was majorly the culprit, the political class and the academy presented the fall-out as being the result of ideological differences. The dominant perception was that these were battles between the left-leaning socialists and pro-capitalists.

Postmodern theory and the postcolonial theory are the buzzwords for the 21st century in the attempt to scrutinize, clarify, and counter to the cultural legacies of colonialism and imperialism. The emphasis is on the politics of knowledge creation, control and distribution that sustain the foreign control of decision-making and value allocation. Some of the key theorists include Frantz Fanon, Edward Said and Gayatri Chakravorty Spivak.

Frantz Fanon (1925-1961) was a well-known critic of imperialism. In *The Wretched of the Earth* (1961), Fanon documents the degrading outcomes of colonization upon the victim and the colonizer. According to Fanon, colonialism and post-colonial legacies are dehumanizing experiences.

Edward Said (1935-2003) contended that Western scholars account of non-Western societies was laced with colonial attitudes of superiority. In *Orientalism* (1978), Said tried to trace the origin and evolution of these condescending slants and representations.

It is strange what relatedness can do. Gayatri Chakravorty Spivak (1942-?) dealt with the dilemma of representation in an attempt to challenge the legacy of colonialism and imperialism. In "Can the Subaltern Speak?", Spivak notes the ambivalence of the voice of sati-performing women forcing her to wonder whether the subaltern can even verbalize their victimhood.

The collapse of the Berlin Wall in 1989 and the subsequent end of the Cold War and with it the Communist dictatorships in Europe and the satellites in Africa and elsewhere in the 1990s ushered in a period of neo-liberal ideas of liberal democracy and market economy. Thereafter, the trend has been widening market relations, broadening democratic practice, constitution making and the value of freedoms.

What is history then? Why we do we seek to understand the past? R. G. Collingwood (1889-1943) in *The Idea of History* (1946) re-assessed how the understanding of why we study the past has changed from the time of Herodotus to the contemporary period to grasp what history really is. He realized that accurate comprehension requires that we unify human experience and knowledge. Collingwood concluded that meaningful historical inquiry must conclude that the goal of history is self-awareness of the mind. History is the study of the mind; the re-enactment of past experience.

Relatedness is a state of mind; a mental attribute. For millennia, relatedness has driven and determined the course and direction of world history. Even then, the story of our past demonstrates that our respective journeys are purpose-driven. History is a record of our past associations and struggles in pursuit of the common objective of survival. Historical connectedness examines how the patterns and processes of world history have drawn peoples of the world together to surmount the travails of life on earth. Connectedness is the journey and destination of history.

INTELLECTUAL CONNECTEDNESS

Mental faculties are non-spatial properties that allow us to view, understand and manipulate the universe. There exists a variety of methodical and practical approaches to acquiring knowledge about the world around us and our relationship with it. Even then, all knowledge systems are often intertwined and dependent on each other. All forms of knowing share a common purpose.

The intellect is the faculty of critical or analytical reasoning to objectively understand and grasp the world. What unites intellectuals in the natural sciences, social sciences and humanities, and practitioners is not the nature and scope of knowledge but the usefulness of acquired knowledge.

Knowledge is conscious. Humans use thought and reason, faith, imagination, intuition, memory and sense experience to connect with the rest of the universe.

Year after year, breakthroughs and advances in science are changing our perception of the universe.

Knowledge plays a vital role in all aspects of our lives. Science has been trying to rewrite the boundaries between life and death. All around the world changes occur on the fringes of comprehension. However, the current near water-tight compartmentalization of the ever-expanding knowledge (the silo approach) may possibly not satisfactorily guarantee our existence.

Human knowledge is responsible for distinctive historical monuments and architectural designs; exploits in engineering; the inventions of fire, tools and cooking; discoveries of early forms of paper, written scripts, the calendar and the printing press; beginnings of sedentary life and shelter constructions; strides in irrigation systems, crop and animal husbandry; invention of the wheel, exploration and transportation; the invention of zero (and other numerals) that have helped simplify mathematical calculations; the discovery of the telescope, plate tectonics and optics; the emergence of urban life; and many other great advances.

Scientists hope to create positive change in the world through discoveries and innovations. The intellectual momentum of science must be premised on the needs, aspirations and goals of society. However, intellectual and technological change directed by political causes (relatedness) inevitably influence what science gets done but often fails to advance the interests of the world society as a whole.

Intellectual connectedness requires cooperation, collaboration and knowledge sharing between and across disciplines. This is because the scientific enterprise as a whole is about the purpose not the method. However, most scientific disciplines have increasingly become methodical and exclusive (in terms of appropriate sources, methodologies and theories) and less about the purpose (impact and audience).

Intellectual connectedness can change the direction of the way we relate with our natural and social surroundings.

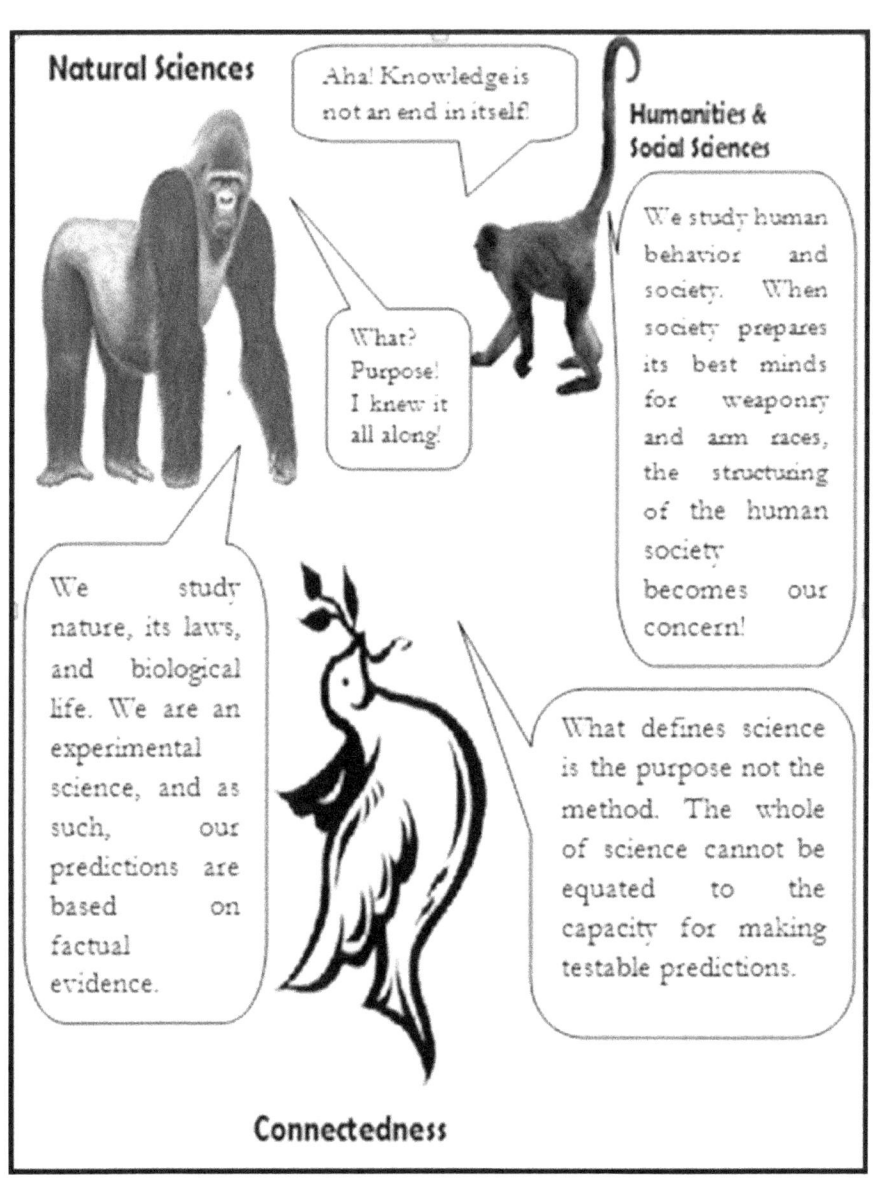

Fig. 8: The Ultimate Rapprochement

Source: Khamala (2014b)

CONCLUSION

Connectedness shifts our understanding of the universe. Connectedness is where the whole is greater than the sum of its parts. Connectedness as evidenced in our everyday experience (and as a thought process) presents the universe in one wholesome piece while also demonstrating how and why it appears to us in the form of isolated components.

CHAPTER FOUR

CONCLUSION

This work has demonstrated why and how globalization (a form of relatedness) is being replaced by connectedness.

Connectedness (inclusiveness) is a superior approach to global integration as compared to globalization (exclusiveness) which is a form of imperialism.

Relatedness is a deeply flawed paradigm that habitually encourages individuals to act knowingly or unknowingly against their own and collective interest. Relatedness is also a drag on intellectual discourse and the search for practical solutions to problems afflicting world society as it leads to less-than optimal resource utilization.

Global togetherness represents a sustainable form of global integration made possible by increased human awareness of a shared value system, a common cause and an attachment to our natural and social surroundings.

Networks of urbanized neighborhoods are the new fronts for global integration. The nonprofit sector can be tasked to encourage interaction, dialogue, consultation, knowledge sharing and collaboration worldwide.

In a connectedness world, leading a meaningful life is the ultimate goal.

It is time to embrace value systems that appreciate the meaningfulness of human interaction

social contact loneliness and social isolation

BIBLIOGRAPHY

Amin Samir (2001*). Imperialism and Globalization.* New York: Monthly Review Press.

Antognazza Maria Rosa (2008). *Leibniz: An Intellectual Biography.* Cambridge University Press.

Aristotle (350 BCE). *Physics.* Hardie RP, Gaye RK (Trans). Retrieved 26 December 2013 from http://classics.mit.edu/Aristotle/physics.html.

Bakan Joel (2005). *The Corporation: The Pathological Pursuit of Profit and Power.* New York: Free Press.

Bauer Susan Wise (2010). *The History of the Medieval World: From the Conversion of Constantine to the First Crusade.* New York: W. W. Norton.

Bransden, B. H.; Joachain, CJ (2003). *Physics of Atoms and Molecules.* Prentice Hall.

Carr Benard (ed.) (2007). *Universe or Multiverse?* Cambridge University Press.

Chivers CJ (2013). "Mikhail Kalashnikov, Creator of AK-47, Dies at 94". *The New York Times,* 23 December, 2013.

Chomsky Naom (2003). *Hegemony or Survival: America's Quest for Global Dominance*. Metropolitan Books.

Darwin Charles (1859). *On the Origin of Species by Means of Natural Selection, or the Preservation of Favoured Races in the Struggle for Life*. London: John Murray.

Dawkins Richard (1976). *The Selfish Gene*. Oxford: Oxford University Press.

De Waal FBM (2008). "Putting the altruism back into altruism: The evolution of empathy". *Annual Review of Psychology* 59: 279–300.

Einstein A, Podolsky B, and Rosen N (1935). "Can quantum-mechanical description of physical reality be considered complete?" *Physical Review* Volume 47, 777-780.

Einstein Albert (2010). *Relativity: The Special and the General Theory*. Robert W, Lawson RL (Trans). Andras Nagy.

Ellis J (2000). "There's a place for the theory of everything". *Nature* 403, 241-242.

El-Rabbany Ahmed (2002). *Introduction to GPS: The Global Positioning System*. Artech house, Inc.

Euclid (2002). *Euclid's Elements*. Heath TL and Densmore D (Trans). Green Lion Press.

Fant Kenne (1991) [2006]. *Alfred Nobel: A Biography*. Transl. Ruth Marianne. New York: Arcade Publishing.

Freud Sigmund (2001). *The Complete Psychological Works*. Strachey J (ed). Vintage Paperbacks.

Fukuyama Francis (1992). *The End of History and the Last Man*. New York: Free Press.

Grayling AC (2005). *Descartes: The Life and times of a Genius*. New York: Walker Publishing Co., Inc.

Greene Robert (1998) [2000]. *The 48 Laws of Power*. Penguin Books.

Hosseini SA Hamed (2009). Global Complexities and the Rise of Global Justice Movement: A New Notion of Justice. *The Global Studies Journal* 2 (3): 15–36.

Juris Jeffreys S. (2008) *Networking Futures: The Movements against Corporate Globalization*. Durham: Duke University Press.

Khamala Geoffreyson (2009) *Gender Dimension of Ethnic Conflicts in Kenya: The Case of Bukusu and Sabaot Communities.* MA Thesis, Kenyatta University, Kenya.

Khamala Geoffreyson (2014a). *The Perfect Theory: A Complete Unified Description of the Universe.* Tajiriba Foundation.

Khamala Geoffreyson (2014b). *What is Science! Science as an Adaptive Capacity.* Tajiriba Foundation.

Khamala Geoffreyson (2014c). *Is Science Religion.* Tajiriba Foundation.

Kohn Alfie (1992). *No Contest: The Case Against Competition.* Houghton Mifflin Harcourt.

Machiavelli Niccolò (1532) [2003]. The Prince. Dante University Press.

Marshall Michael (2010). Knowing the mind of God: Seven theories of everything. *NewScientist.* Retrieved Available   at: http://www.newscientist.com/article/dn18612-knowing-the-mind-of-god-seven-theories-of-everything.html?

Monk Ray (2013) *Robert Oppenheimer: His Life and Mind.* Random House.

Morgenthau Hans (1948) *Politics Among Nations: The Struggle for Power and Peace.* New York NY: Alfred A. Knopf.

Musser George (2008). *The Complete Idiot's Guide to String Theory.* Alpha.

Musser George (2013). What Happens to Google Maps When Tectonic Plates Move? In: *ScientificAmerica*n. Retrieved on 12 December 2013 from: http://blogs.scientificamerican.com/critical-opalescence/2013/11/11/what-happens-to-google-maps-when-tectonic-plates-move/.

Nicolson Iain (2007). *Dark Side of the Universe: Dark Matter, Dark Energy, and the Fate of the Cosmos.* Johns Hopkins University Press.

Nilesh V, Manapat ML, Chen IA, et al (2012). "Spontaneous network formation among cooperative RNA replicators". *Nature* 491, 72–77.

Nobelprize.org (2014). Alfred Nobel: The Man Behind the Nobel Prizes. Retrieved on Monday, November 24, 2014 from http://www.nobelprize.org/alfred_nobel/

Panek Richard (2012). *The 4 Percent Universe: Dark Matter, Dark Energy, and the Race to Discover the Rest of Reality.* Mariner Books.

Perkins John (2004). *Confessions of an Economic Hit Man.* San Francisco, California: Berrett-Koehler.

Perlmutter S, Aldering G, Goldhaber G et al (The Supernova Cosmology Project) (1999). "Measurements of Omega and Lambda from 42 High Redshift Supernovae". *Astrophysical Journal* 517 (2): 565–86.

Piraino S, Boero F, Aeschbach B, Schmid V (1996). "Reversing the Life Cycle: Medusae Transforming into Polyps and Cell Transdifferentiation in Turritopsis nutricula (Cnidaria, Hydrozoa)". *Biological Bulletin* 190 (3): 302–312.

Pollack Gerald L. & Stump Daniel R. (2001). *Electromagnetism.* Addison-Wesley.

Pumfrey Stephen (2002). William Gilbert. In Harman P, Mitton S (eds) *Cambridge Scientific Minds.* Cambridge University Press, pp.6-20.

Rousseau Jean-Jacques (2012). *The Social Contract.* Retrieved on 29 December 2013 from:

http://ebooks.adelaide.edu.au/r/rousseau/jean_jacqu es/r864s/index.html.

Samir Amin (2001). "Imperialism and Globalization". *Monthly Review*, Volume 53, Issue 02 (June).

Sassen Saskia (2003). "Globalization or Denationalisation?" *Review of International Political Economy* 10:1 February 2003: 1–22. Routledge.

Schopenhauer Arthur (1958). *The World as Will and Representation*. Falcon's Wing Press.

Schrödinger Erwin (2012). *What Is Life? Mind and Matter*. Cambridge University Press.

Seifer Marc (1996). *The Life and Times of Nikola Tesla: Biography of a Genius*. Citadel Press.

Selleri F (1988). *Quantum Mechanics Versus Local Realism: The Einstein–Podolsky–Rosen Paradox*. New York: Plenum Press.

Spellerberg Anne (2001). *Framework for the measurement of social capital in New Zealand*. Research and Analytical Report no.14. Wellington: Statistics New Zealand.

Stiglitz Joseph (2003). *Globalization and its Discontents*. W. W. Norton & Company.

Tipler Frank (1997). *The Physics of Immortality: Modern Cosmology, God and the Resurrection of the Dead*. Anchor.

Waltz Kenneth (2000). "Globalization and American Power". *National Interest*: 59: 46-56.

Weinberg Steven (1993). *Dreams of a Final Theory: The Search for the Fundamental Laws of Nature*. London: Hutchinson Radius.

Westfall Richard S. (2007). *Isaac Newton*. Cambridge University Press.

Wheeler JCraig (2007). *Cosmic Catastrophes*. Cambridge University Press.

Wilson Edward O (1971). *The Insect Societies*. Cambridge, Massachusetts: Belknap Press of Harvard University Press.

Darwin John (2008). *After Tamerlane: The Rise and Fall of Global Empires, 1400–2000*. Penguin Books.

Ferguson Niall (2004). *Empire: How Britain Made the Modern World*. Penguin Books.

Gilbert, Erik and Reynolds, Jonathan T. (2008). *Africa in World History: From Prehistory to the Present.* Upper Saddle River: Pearson.

Hobsbawm E. J. (1989). *The Age of Empire, 1875–1914.* Abacus Books.

Hobsbawm E. J. (2008). *On Empire: America, War, and Global Supremacy.* Pantheon Books.

Hobson J. A. (2005). *Imperialism: A Study.* Cosimo Classics.

Joseph A. Schumpeter (1918). The Sociology of Imperialism

Lenin Vladimir Illyich (2000). *Imperialism, the Highest Phase of Capitalism.* Delhi: Leftword Books.

Prabhat Patnaik (2005). "The Economics of the New Phase of Imperialism", at www.networkideas.org

Said Edward (1998). *Culture and Imperialism.* Vintage Books.

Lenin Vladimir (1997). *Imperialism: The Highest Stage of Capitalism.* New York New York: International Publishers.

Smolin Lee (2007). *The Trouble With Physics: The Rise of String Theory, The Fall of a Science, and What Comes Next.* Mariner Books.

Ackah, William B. (1999). *Pan-Africanism: Exploring the Contradictions, Politics, Identity and Development in Africa and the African Diaspora.* Brookfield, Vt.: Ashgate.

Esedebe, P. Olisanwuche (1994). *Pan-Africanism: The Idea and Movement, 1776-1991.* Washington, D.C.: Howard University.

Walters, Ronald W. (1993). *Pan-Africanism in the African Diaspora: An Analysis of Modern Afrocentric Political Movements.* Detroit, Mich.: Wayne State.

Mazrui Ali A. (Ed.) (1999). *UNESCO General History of Africa, Vol. VIII: Africa since 1935.* London: James Currey.

Ki-Zerbo, J., (ed.) (1990). *UNESCO General History of Africa, Vol. 1, Methodology and African Prehistory.* Berkeley: University of California Press.

Ogot B.A. (1999). *UNESCO General History of Africa, Vol. V: Africa from the Sixteenth to the Eighteenth Century.* Berkeley: University of California Press.

Sharman Fergus (2013). *Linguistic Ties Between Ancient Egyptian and Bantu: Uncovering Symbiotic Affinities and Relationships in Vocabulary.* Universal Publishers.

Johnson Paul (1979) [1976]. *History of Christianity*. Simon & Schuster.

Bede (1990) [731]. *Ecclesiastical History of the English People*. Penguin Classics.

History of Christianity. Retrieved on Friday, January 02, 2015 from http://en.wikipedia.org/wiki/History_of_Christianity.

Marx Karl (2011) [1867]. *Das Kapital*. Trans. Samuel Moore. CreateSpace Independent Publishing Platform.

Marx Karl (2012) [1859]. *A Contribution to the Critique of Political Economy*. Forgotten Books.

Marx Karl and Engels Fredriech (2004) [1848]. *The Communist Manifesto*. Penguin.

Lenin V. I. (1969) [1917]. *Imperialism: The Highest Stage of Capitalism, A Popular Outline*. New York: International Publishers.

Amin S. (1976), 'Unequal Development: An Essay on the Social Formations of Peripheral Capitalism' New York: Monthly Review Press.

Baran, P and Sweezy, P. (1966). "Monopoly Capital: An essay on the American economic and social order." New York. Monthly Review Press.

Cardoso, F. H. and Faletto, E. (1979), 'Dependency and development in Latin América'. University of California Press.

Baran Paul A. (1957). *The Political Economy of Growth*. New York: Monthly Review Press. pp. 22–23, 41–42.

Frank Andre Gunder (1967). *Capitalism and Underdevelopment in Latin America*. New York: Monthly Review Press.

Frank Andre Gunder (1979). *Dependent Accumulation and Underdevelopment*. New York: Monthly Review Press.

Amin Samir (1974). *Accumulation on a World Scale*. New York: Monthly Review Press.

Cardoso Fernando Henrique (1977). "The Consumption of Dependency Theory in the United States," *Latin American Research Review* 12, no. 3 (1977): 19–20.

Rostow Walt (1960). *The Stages of Economic Growth: A Non-Communist Manifesto*. Cambridge: Cambridge University Press.

Amin Samir (1976). *Unequal Development: An Essay on the Social Formations of Peripheral Capitalism*. Trans. Brian Pearce. New York: Monthly Review Press.

Amin Samir (1977). *Imperialism and Unequal Development*. New York: Monthly Review Press.

Wallerstein Immanuel (2004). *World-Systems Analysis: An Introduction*. Duke University Press.

Wallerstein Immanuel (1974). *The Modern World System: Capitalist Agriculture and the Origins of the European World Economy in the Sixteenth Century*. New York: Academic Press.

Hegel G. W. F. (1976) [1806]. *Phenomenology of Spirit*. Trans. A. V. Miller. Oxford University Press.

Hegel G. W. F. (2004). [1821]. *The Philosophy of History*. Trans. J. Sibree. Dover Publications.

Hegel G. W. F. (2014). *Hegel's Philosophy of Mind*. Trans. William Wallace. CreateSpace Independent Publishing Platform.

Fanon, Frantz (2005) [1961]. *The Wretched of the Earth*. New York: Grove Press.

Said, Edward (1978). *Orientalism*. New York: Pantheon.

Spivak, Gayatri Chakravorty (1990).

Sharp, J. (2008). "Chapter 6, Can the Subaltern Speak?". Geographies of Postcolonialism. SAGE Publications.

Collingwood R.G. (1994) [1946]. *The Idea of History*. Oxford University Press.

Hanson Victor Davis (2006). *A War Like No Other: How the Athenians and Spartans Fought the Peloponnesian War*. New York: Random House.

Herodotus (440 BCE). *The History of Herodotus*. Retrieved on Monday, January 05, 2015 from http://classics.mit.edu/Herodotus/history.html.

Al-Djazairi S.E. (2006). *The Golden Age and Decline of Islamic Civilisation*. Bayt Al-Hikma Press.

Lombard Maurice (2003). *The Golden Age of Islam*. Markus Wiener Pub.

Khaldûn Ibn (2004) [406]. *The Muqaddimah: An Introduction to History*. Trans. Franz Rosenthal. Princeton University Press.

www.ingramcontent.com/pod-product-compliance
Lightning Source LLC
Chambersburg PA
CBHW060627290526
45793CB00001B/169